Quick and Easy, Proven Recipes

Caribbean Cooking

Publisher's Note: Raw or semi-cooked eggs should not be consumed by babies, toddlers, pregnant or breastfeeding women, the elderly or those suffering from a chronic illness.

Publisher & Creative Director: Nick Wells
Senior Project Editor: Catherine Taylor
Art Director: Mike Spender
Layout Design: Jane Ashley
Digital Design & Production: Chris Herbert

Special thanks to Esme Chapman and Frances Bodiam.

This is a **FLAME TREE** Book

FLAME TREE PUBLISHING
Crabtree Hall, Crabtree Lane
Fulham, London SW6 6TY
United Kingdom
www.flametreepublishing.com

First published 2014

14 16 18 17 15
1 3 5 4 2

ISBN: 978-1-78361-244-4

A copy of the CIP data for this book is available from the British Library.

Printed in Singapore

All recipe photographs courtesy of Flame Tree Publishing Ltd except the following, which are courtesy of Practical Pictures, © Anness Publishing Ltd: 66, 68 178; **and Shutterstock:** 90, 124, 146, 190, 218, 222, 224, 228, 240.

Non-recipe photographs courtesy of the following:
Shutterstock: 4, 7–10, 13, 16–19, 22–25, 27, 30–33, 35, 37, 44–45, 50–52, 54–55. **Fotolia:** 6, 11, 21, 36, 39–40, 47. **iStockphoto:** 20, 26, 28–29, 34, 38, 41–42, 46, 48–49, 53. **Topham Picturepoint:** 43.

Quick and Easy, Proven Recipes

Caribbean Cooking

FLAME TREE PUBLISHING

Contents

Introduction

č

Picture ivory-white sandy beaches, palm trees dipping their fronds into crystalline turquoise waters and sailboats lazily drifting to shore – and you will be conjuring up a Caribbean paradise. Yet it is the sight, aroma and taste sensations of well-prepared food that are most evocative of times and places, and revitalize memories in a way that photographs can never recapture.

Whether the Caribbean is familiar to you or not, you can explore the region's culinary delights and begin to uncover the many pleasures of Caribbean food through these pages. The story of Caribbean food, however, is not a simple one. Like the islands themselves, the peoples of the Caribbean are united in the tangled web of their combined histories. Their cultures of dance, art, music and cuisine all reflect a complex heritage that owes a debt to the present-day inhabitants and their forebears, who often faced great adversity and times of hardship.

The early inhabitants of the islands – Amerindians and Caribs – brought food and recipes from the Americas. When Christopher Columbus toured the region in the late fifteenth century, his Spanish forces were the vanguard of a huge European movement that wanted to colonize the Caribbean, and exploit its rich reserves of natural resources. The European powers battled for centuries over the various territories, each wanting to increase its hold in the region. They caused turmoil, instability and loss of life

while doing so. Islands were passed between French, British, Spanish, Dutch and Portuguese hands following many bloody battles.

African slaves, mostly from the Gold Coast, were shipped to the islands in their thousands to work the sugar plantations, and migrants from Asia came to seek their fortunes in prospering economies. With each wave of immigration came new ingredients, ideas and inspiration – and recipes gradually evolved, usually passed from mother to daughter by word of mouth. Now, a single Caribbean menu may display this rich tapestry of cuisine with listings of Creole jerk chicken, Indian curried goat and an Indonesian rice table. The variety of dishes on offer certainly gives a fascinating insight into the region's unsettled history.

Fruits of the Soil

Not all Caribbean islands are fertile, but most of them can be cultivated to some degree. Enjoying a tropical climate, the region benefits from both sunshine and rain, and many islands are verdant, lush places where mango and papaya trees line the earthen tracks and tarmac roads. It is not unusual to see mango trees so laden with ripe fruits that the mangoes fall to the ground before anyone – except the enthralled tourist – notices them. Sugar cane was once the dominant crop on many islands; it is still grown extensively (and used not just to produce sugar, but molasses and rum, too). Pineapples are native to Jamaica, and these tropical fruits were sent to Hawaii – but other plants were introduced to the region from elsewhere, and have become firmly established in both the soil and the cuisine. Bananas, Bombay mangoes, and citrus trees are all immigrants; the popular breadfruit was introduced to Jamaica by Captain Bligh, of mutiny fame. Okra, an important plant in Caribbean cooking, was

imported by African slaves and is used as a vegetable and a thickener.

Fruits of the Sea

Visitors to the Caribbean naturally gravitate to the coast, where beautiful vistas can be enjoyed from a beachside tavern or restaurant, while sampling the delicious fruits of the sea. Fish and shellfish, of course, play an important role in Caribbean cuisine. The clear waters of the Caribbean Sea and Atlantic Ocean offer a range of delights to the fish chef; from sea urchins, conch and octopus to grouper, snapper and marlin. Fish soups and chowders are common throughout the Caribbean; with a smattering of locally grown vegetables and the addition of herbs and spices, each island produces a unique version.

As with all nations that rely heavily on fish and shellfish for protein, Caribbean islanders are increasingly aware of the problems of over-fishing. Fishing seasons are being established in some areas to protect fish, turtle and conch stocks, and the resourceful Caribbean islanders are substituting some common species for those that are in decline. Fish recipes generally can be easily adapted to suit the fish that is available to the cook.

Spices & Seasonings

Caribbean food is rarely bland in colour or flavour. The simple food staples of African slaves were turned into lively meals by the addition of spices, borrowing ideas from the Spanish,

French, Indians and Chinese. Starchy root vegetables such as cassava or potato are spiced up with a splash of hot pepper sauce or sprinkling of cayenne. The most famous of all Caribbean seasonings, however, is Jamaican jerk. The fiery, spicy mixture contains allspice and Scotch bonnet peppers, which are among the hottest available. Cloves, cinnamon, garlic, nutmeg and thyme are some of the other ingredients added to the blend. The paste is rubbed into the meat before cooking, ideally over wood or charcoal.

Pleasure is an integral part of the Caribbean way of life. Hassle, hustle and haste simply don't feature; enjoyment of food is part and parcel of this laconic, laid-back lifestyle. Islanders may be aware that fried treats from street vendors, such as fritters, are not the healthiest of foods, but they take the view that all things are fine in moderation – and get on with enjoying the sensations of taste and smell.

Many Caribbean recipes may appear complex because of the numbers of spices or herbs involved, but in reality they can all be prepared at a leisurely pace, and stews and soups often benefit from long, gentle cooking; frenetically prepared food is not the Caribbean approach. Gentle stewing allows flavours from the seasoning to infuse, and the cook can add a little more from time to time, until the meat reaches a point of perfect succulence. The cooking pot, rather like the Caribbean itself, benefits from a heady mix of different ingredients, which come together over time, to blend into something entirely new and wonderful.

Landscapes *and* Culture

Known for its crystal clear waters and vibrant culture, the Caribbean is an island region like no other. Before you get stuck in to the range of delicious food and drink recipes this book has to offer, sit back and immerse yourself in the unique traditions and stunning landscapes captured in this chapter. From the majestic mountains of Hispaniola to the banana plantations of Dominica, discover local quirks and tasty specialities of each island and wish yourself away to that sun-drenched beach.

The Bahamas

The Bahamas are a large group of more than 700 islands and tiny coral cays, stretching in an archipelago over 100,000 square miles (260,000 square kilometres) in the Atlantic Ocean. The inhabited islands have an exceptionally strong European and American influence, due in part to their close proximity to Florida. Despite problems associated with poverty (like most of the Caribbean), the Bahamas are among the wealthiest of all the Caribbean islands, with an income derived from a healthy tourist trade and a flourishing financial services industry.

The islands came under British rule in 1718, and remained relatively stable politically from there on, gaining full independence from Britain in 1973. Their food, however, is truly international, with worldwide influences. While some foods are treated with a delicate touch, others are doused in fiery pepper sauces – for the cuisine of the Bahamas has been greatly influenced by the American South.

Local seafood is a staple, being plentiful in the turquoise crystal-clear waters that surround the islands. Dishes with crayfish are a fine example of Bahamian cuisine served minced, boiled or added to salads. Conch (pronounced 'konk') is a shellfish with firm, tasty meat that is often added to chowders, or sprinkled with lime juice and spices before frying, making a popular bite-sized bar snack. Land crabs can be seen scuttling across roads at dusk, and are particularly delicious boiled or baked. Locally available fish include red snapper, yellowtail and grouper, which is boiled to maintain its delicate flavour and flaky texture. Rice or grits are often served with fish and crab dishes, with macaroni and cheese, or potato salad. The islands are strewn with coconut trees, and coconut milk and flesh are used liberally in many recipes.

Cuba

ℓ

ew islands in the Caribbean evoke the complex atmosphere of Latin American excitement, exuberance and sheer hardship as vividly as Cuba. With its traumatic history and politics, this island, which is the largest of the Greater Antilles, has captivated and fascinated acclaimed writers such as Ernest Hemingway and Pedro Juan Gutiérrez, and inspired great artists such as Jean-Baptiste Vermay. The Cuban people have an extraordinary ability to survive; in the recent past the island has been the stage for corruption, communist revolution, crime waves and great poverty. Nevertheless, the resilient people are able to lay their worries to one side and celebrate life with carnival, great food, vibrant music and dance, such as the rumba, cha cha, salsa and danzón.

The Cubans are less enamoured of the spicy chillies and curries found in such abundance elsewhere in the Caribbean. Like those of neighbouring islands, Cuba's cultural heritage is a mixture of influences, which all contribute flavours, colours and textures to the nation's cuisine. African, Arabic, Portuguese, Spanish, Creole and Chinese immigrants have all added to Cuban food. For historical reasons, however, there is considerable regionality in the traditional cuisine. *Comida criolla* (Creole cooking), for example, is found mostly in the east.

The main ingredient for most traditional dishes is a sauté of green peppers, onions, garlic and bay leaves, called 'sofrito', and olive oil is liberally used to cook meat, poultry, fish and vegetables. Dishes are rarely deep-fried; sautéing and slow cooking are the preferred methods, allowing cooks to be more leisurely in the kitchen and to continually adjust the seasoning until the point of perfection is reached. Cuban meat dishes, in particular, are famous for their rich marinades and slow cooking, which combine to produce melt-in-the-mouth tenderness.

Jamaica

The huge depth and variety of Jamaica's culinary delights owes much to the size of the island. For this is the third-largest Caribbean island and, with an area of more than 1,500 square kilometres, it is one of the few islands that is able to sustain agriculture on a commercial level.

The islanders are less dependent on imported food than many of their neighbours, and have become experts at using local produce to create a rich and diverse range of dishes. There are some large-scale orchards on the island, but it is the smaller farmers who dominate the agricultural landscape, producing mixed crops of colourful fruit and vegetables, such as mangoes, bananas, limes, avocados and sugar cane. In the cooler mountain region, green crops of lettuce, cabbage, pak choi, spring onions and herbs do well. While many of the crops are indigenous, the huge range owes much to the efforts of immigrants who have, over centuries, introduced new varieties of plants to the island.

The cultural roots of Jamaica are steeped in a complex history that has seen the integration of many peoples, including Amerindians, African slaves and colonizing Europeans. Each new wave of immigration has brought fresh ideas to the cooking pot. The result is a heady, vibrant and exciting blend of tangy tropical fruit, burning chillies and spicy curries. Spicy goat curries, sweet and sour pork, salted cod, stewed peas and jerked meat might be accompanied by carbohydrate-rich foods such as rice, yams and cassava. Banana loaf, banana fritters, tropical fruit salad and coconut ice cream are all perfect ways to finish off a traditional Jamaican meal. With such an array of flavours and colours to tempt the palate, it is no surprise that visitors to Jamaica return home enthused and inspired to re-create their favourite dishes in their own kitchens.

Hispaniola

&

One of the most beautiful and culturally rich islands in the Greater Antilles, Hispaniola has had a chequered past. Its name, derived from La Isla Española, which means the Spanish Island, bears testament to the conquering powers of the Spanish in the fifteenth and sixteenth centuries, when they held sway over much of the Caribbean region. Hispaniola was first brought to the attention of Europeans by Christopher Columbus, who visited the island four times and, enraptured by the turquoise seas, majestic mountainous regions and beaches of golden sand, declared: 'There is no more beautiful island in the world.'

The indigenous Amerindians lived on the island for some 5,000 years; their ethnic roots were probably both Central and South American. A peaceful people, the Taíno Amerindians were virtually annihilated by the beginning of the seventeenth century, as the Spanish, who killed with impunity, and bearing diseases to which the Indians had no immunity, sought to strip the island of its gold. Years of fighting and unrest followed, as French colonists took over parts of the western side of the island and established sugar plantations, worked by African slaves. Revolution led to the formation of the republic of Haiti. By 1844, the Dominican Republic was formed, occupying two-thirds of the island. Fighting between the two neighbours raged, and the story of violence, unrest and hardship in Haiti and the Dominican Republic continues into modern times. Recently, the Dominican Republic has benefited from a huge growth in tourism, and has become more economically and politically stable, once again earning its right to be known as the paradise that enthralled Christopher Columbus.

In the modern Hispaniola, cuisine bears the hallmarks of Spanish and African influences and, as in neighbouring Cuba, a sofrito is the ubiquitous base of many dishes. Simple meals of fish, meat, rice and salad are enjoyed by families and tourists, who are now able to participate in the delights of a Hispaniolan kitchen.

Puerto Rico

Of all the Caribbean islands, Puerto Rico has a reputation of having maintained the strongest Spanish influence. It is the most easterly of the Greater Antilles and steeped in tradition; the city of Old San Juan, for example, was first built as a fortress and is still peppered with fifteenth-century buildings, such as the gun tower pictured to the left.

The Spaniards managed to maintain control of the island for hundreds of years, despite attempts by the British, French and Dutch to rout them. As a result of the Spanish-American War, Puerto Rico was ceded to the United States and now enjoys its status as a self-governing commonwealth.

Despite its long relationship with Spain, Puerto Rico – like other Caribbean islands – has become a melting pot of race, culture and religion. African slaves, Chinese and European immigrants, Cubans and others have all sought new lives on the island over 500 years, resulting in a mingling of culinary styles, and imported ingredients, which are almost a signature of Caribbean cooking. It is believed that indigenous Indians cooked with corn, seafood and fruit, but the conquering Spanish introduced sugar cane, pork, beef, rice and olive oil. African slaves brought okra and taro.

Modern Puerto Ricans blend these ingredients with aplomb, creating an enormous variety of dishes that are often colourful and strongly aromatic. Meats are coated in a paste of 'adobo', which is made by crushing oregano, garlic, pepper, salt and peppercorns with olive oil and lime juice or vinegar. The adobo is thoroughly rubbed into the meat, which is then roasted, releasing an appetizing aroma as it cooks. Annatoo seeds are often added to Puerto Rican rice, stews and soups to give them a characteristic yellow colour. A particular festive favourite on the island is whole roasted pig, which is coated with sour orange juice before being barbecued and served with roasted green plantain and a sour garlic sauce.

Cayman Islands

The delightful Cayman Islands have much to offer tourists, but their culinary heritage is limited. These three islands of the Greater Antilles (Grand Cayman, pictured right, Little Cayman and Cayman Brac) have maintained strong links with Britain, Jamaica and the United States since they were first colonized, and they have not had the intimate relationship with the Spanish, Creole and French cultures which has benefited the cuisine of other Caribbean islands. Until the seventeenth century, the Caymans were largely uninhabited, and thereafter the most frequent visitors were shipwrecked sailors, pirates, deserters from the English Civil War and refugees.

Most modern-day Caymanians are of African, British or mixed Afro-British descent, and Jamaican influences dominate many dishes. Conch, a shellfish found in the sparkling shallow waters that surround the islands, is a staple and features in soups, stews and salads. Jerk seasonings are popular, and a traditional dessert of cake that has been soaked with locally made rum is a particular speciality. Tuna and marlin are found in deep waters nearby, but grouper and snapper are more common, and are used in soups or served with tomatoes, peppers and onions.

The development of a vernacular cooking style has been further impeded by the Islands' poor natural resources; agriculture is minimal and, although Caymanians enjoy one of the world's highest standards of living, 90 per cent of all foodstuffs are imported. Curiously, however, it was the availability of a particular type of food that first drew early travellers to the islands: marine turtles. In fact, Christopher Columbus first named the islands Las Tortugas after these large reptiles, which were common in the surrounding waters. (The islands were later renamed the Caymans after the caiman – a rare marine crocodile found in the region.) Subsequent over-exploitation of the Cayman Island green turtle population by fishermen nearly led to their demise, and they remain an endangered species worldwide.

Turks & Caicos Islands

At the tail end of the Bahamian archipelago of the Greater Antilles, a collection of more than 40 tropical islands and cays are sprinkled amidst a dazzling turquoise ocean. The crown colony of Turks and Caicos, like the Bahamas, was formed as part of a geological process that left these coral islands exposed above the sea when water levels dropped. The name 'caicos' is believed to derive from the Spanish word cayos, which means string of islands. These islands are composed of pale, flat rock and are encompassed by enormous stretches of fine ivory-white sand.

As agricultural opportunities are limited, the islanders rely heavily on the fruits of the sea, such as lobster and conch – the latter is often prepared with chopped onion and sweet peppers, lime juice and hot pepper sauce.

The first inhabitants of the islands were Amerindians, who lived peacefully, farming the land, until Europeans arrived in the late fifteenth century. Over the centuries, this small group of islands was ruled by the Bermudans, who established a salt industry here, the Spanish, the French, the Jamaicans and the British.

Today, only 10 of the islands are inhabited, by fewer than 25,000 inhabitants. The population is swelled, however, by the ever-growing numbers of tourists who come to sample a Caribbean paradise. Local dishes include beef patties, which are made from pastry prepared with turmeric, and lean fried beef cooked with curry powder and green onions. Sauce for barbecued spare ribs, which feature prominently on menus around the Caribbean, is prepared in the Turks and Caicos using corn syrup, molasses, brown sugar and plenty of herbs and spices. The flavours in the mixture are allowed to infuse overnight before being poured thickly over pork ribs.

The Virgin Islands

Scattered in a crystal-blue sea and part of the Leeward Islands of the Lesser Antilles, the Virgin Islands are renowned for their secluded beaches and isolated bays. These hideaways, in times past, provided an ideal place for pirates to lurk while waiting for passing cargo ships to plunder. There are around 90 islands altogether in the group, which are formed from the peaks of a row of submerged volcanoes which exploded from the ocean floor some 25 million years ago. British colonists developed large parts of the islands into sugar plantations, and about 50 islands and cays today form the British Virgin Islands (BVI), still retaining close links with Britain. Some of the remaining islands were known as the Danish West Indies until the First World War, when the United States bought the territory from Denmark to prevent the Germans from using the islands as a U-boat base. They now form the United States Virgin Islands.

The cultural heritage of the Virgin Islands pays testament to the thousands of African slaves who were brought to the region to work on the sugar plantations. Many of them were taken from the African Gold Coast, and some modern-day islanders can trace their roots back 300 years. The islands have a palpable Afro-Caribbean flavour, and food reflects the basic diet of sweet potato, okra, breads and cornmeal that were staples for slaves. Fresh fish is a favourite, and local varieties such as wahoo, yellowtail, grouper and red snapper – served with a hot lime sauce – are considered specialities. Virgin Island soups are, unusually, often flavoured with fruit and sweetened with sugar; the most famous soup is callaloo, which is made with a leafy vegetable similar to spinach.

Anguilla, Antigua & Barbuda

resh lobsters, crayfish, yellowtail, whelks and red snapper are just some of the seafood enjoyed on the Leeward island of Anguilla, although here – as on many other Caribbean islands – fruit and vegetables to accompany the fish are often imported. This small island, a self-governing overseas territory of the United Kingdom, has a dry tropical climate, and its erratic rainfall makes agriculture difficult. Natural resources are few, but the inhabitants, who are mostly of African slave descent, have a reputation for being able to create some of the most elegant dishes in the region.

In the Leeward Islands of Antigua and Barbuda, the cuisine is noticeably spicier and more varied. The dishes display some Creole influences, despite these islands' long relationship with Britain, when large sugar-cane plantations were scattered across the interior of Antigua. Sauces may be pepper-hot, or spiced with curry powders from East India. Curried goat and spare ribs are perennial favourites on the islands, and may be served with breadfruit, yams or potatoes. A traditional dish is pepper pot: a spicy, tender stew of beef, pork and dumplings with okra. It is often served with fungi, an accompaniment made of cornmeal and okra, moulded into balls.

As elsewhere in the Caribbean, fried plantains appear on many menus; these vegetables are similar in appearance to bananas, but taste bitter and must be cooked before eating. They can be baked in the oven, or treated in much the same way as potatoes: mashed, fried or boiled. (On Spanish-speaking islands, they often appear as *tostones de plátano* and are fried, squashed and fried again until crispy.) Fresh fish feature in the local cuisine and, as grouper and snapper are still common in surrounding waters, they appear in many recipes. Blue marlin is hunted in deep waters, and is served pan-seared with lime juice or in a salad with curried pumpkin.

Dominica, Saint Martin ❦ Environs

I t has been said that the island of Dominica, the southernmost of the Leeward Islands in the Lesser Antilles, is the only place in the Caribbean that might still be recognized by Christopher Columbus if he were to return to the region today.

This is a dense, mountainous place with tropical forests and few sandy beaches to lure tourists and the large hotel operators. The island is lush and fertile, and, although varied fruit and vegetable crops are cultivated here, banana plantations have predominated. The Dominicans have paid a heavy price for this monoculture; when the price of bananas falls, or the crop is damaged by tropical storms, farmers struggle to survive.

French and British influences compete on the island today, but unusually there is a small region of native Carib people, the tribe that had settled on the island (and many others in the region) before Christopher Columbus arrived. As one might expect, the cuisine of Dominica reflects all these cultures, but it also has some rather unusual and distinctive dishes. 'Mountain chicken', for example, is a delicacy made from the flesh of a frog. Land crabs are also popular, and fresh seafood such as octopus, flying fish and spiny lobsters is readily available.

In Saint Martin, Dutch and other European influences have been brought to bear, but more traditional recipes of this Leeward Island include succulent meat curries, seafood seasoned with peppers, and stuffed crab. In Saint Barthélemy, the cuisine is mostly international, and few local dishes survive. Food is, nevertheless, is given a Caribbean lilt with mango sauces or Creole spices. Cuisine in Saba is unremarkable, being mostly continental and relying on imported ingredients. Regional cooking includes fresh seafood.

Montserrat, Saint Kitts & Saint Eustatius

Once known as an emerald island, rich and green, Montserrat sits in the southern range of the Leeward Islands and is, in nature, a verdant tropical island covered with fertile soil, rainforest and lush vegetation.

Its fortunes have changed spectacularly, however, in recent times. In 1995 the volcano of Soufrière burst into life after 350 years of dormancy and began to erupt, producing grey ash that fell over the southern part of the island. It continued its activity, which gradually grew in severity until 1997 – when a huge pyroclastic flow of high-speed lava destroyed seven villages and killed 19 people. Now the island's population is a fraction of what it once was (out of 11,000, only an estimated 4,000 remain). The people of Montserrat still serve their local cuisine the tourists who come to view the active volcano, and the visitors are treated to the national dish of goat stew, known locally as goat water, served with chunks of bread. Frog, also known as 'mountain chicken' is a traditional regional delicacy.

Amongst the Leeward Islands Saint Kitts enjoys a good reputation for its local seafood, which is prepared by traditional Caribbean methods. Pepper pot stew, conch curry and spiny lobster are commonplace. The local drink is a liqueur, made from sugar cane and mixed with grapefruit soda. Traditional dishes of neighbouring Nevis include roasted and spiced suckling pig, and turtle (although this is now discouraged as turtles are endangered). Aubergine and avocados are used liberally.

Known commonly as 'Statia', the little Dutch island of Saint Eustatius is steeped in a history that is being preserved for a burgeoning tourist trade. Its cuisine is varied, reflecting international tastes; Chinese food is particularly popular here, although some traditional Creole and Caribbean dishes are also prepared, such as goat stew. Cheese plays an important part in local recipes, reflecting the influence of Dutch colonizers.

The Leeward French Antilles

Along with Martinique, the islands of Guadeloupe, La Désirade, Les Saintes and Marie-Galante make up the French Antilles, and are unmistakably Gallic in their culture and cuisine. There is, however, the usual potpourri of races in the French Antilles that is found elsewhere in the region; African, East Indian and British migrants have all added to the islands' heritage.

Of these islands, Guadeloupe possibly boasts the most exciting and imaginative of cuisines. Creole flavours dominate; the essence of Creole cooking is a fusion of French, Spanish and African ingredients and methods. The result is a powerful burst of flavour; meats are always well spiced, and sauces often have a tomato, garlic and herb base – there is little tradition of cooking with dairy products. Seafood in Guadeloupe is treated with French delicacy of touch, and local herbs are added to enhance subtle flavours. A regional favourite is callaloo soup, made from leafy greens and herbs, and Colombo is a staple here. This tender meat or poultry stew is made with sweet potato, pumpkin, herbs, spices and rice. It is named after the capital of Sri Lanka – workers migrated from here to tend the sugar plantations, and brought their strong spices with them.

The little islands of La Désirade, Les Saintes and Marie-Galante lie in the warm tropical waters around the larger, busier Guadeloupe. They offer tranquillity, with beautiful beaches and beautiful coral reefs; however, there is little local produce as the landscape is mostly arid with poor soil. Local dishes include court-bouillon – a dish made from poached fish served with lime, wine, potatoes and onion – and accra – balls of locally caught fish and chillies, deep-fried in batter.

Barbados

Part of the Windward Islands of the Lesser Antilles, the Caribbean paradise of Barbados may be known as 'Little England' locally, but its cuisine reflects a far wider range of influences and Bajans owe little to the British in terms of food. The island's first inhabitants were migrants from South America, including the Arawak and Carib Indians, although the island is believed to have been uninhabited by the fifteenth century when the Spanish arrived. The British landed in the 1620s and, uniquely, maintained their rule of this Caribbean island until independence in 1966. Thousands of Africans were brought to Barbados as slaves, and many Celts from Ireland and Scotland migrated to the island to work as servants, all adding to the ethnic mix that now exists on the island.

The island enjoys a tropical climate and, although many areas have been developed and urbanized, areas of wild rainforest, marsh and mangrove swamp survive intact. Sugar cane still dominates much of the agriculture, but a large variety of vegetables and fruits, such as papaya, passion fruit and mango, are grown on the island, sold at the lively markets.

They feature in the culinary delights on offer to both locals and the many tourists who visit this popular island. Rum and molasses are by-products of the sugar cane, and these have come to feature in Bajan dishes. Traditional fare includes the ubiquitous flying fish, which is served in a variety of ways, including boiled, stewed and fried. Cooked well, it is moist and has a delicate nutty flavour, and it is often served with a yellow sauce of mustard and onions. A store cupboard essential is the Bajan seasoning mix, made from a blend of chopped onions, Scotch bonnet peppers and garlic mixed with herbs, seasoning, vinegar and Worcestershire sauce. This seasoning is left for a week to mature, before being rubbed on meat, poultry or fish.

Grenada, Martinique, Saint Lucia ⚘ Saint Vincent

P art of the Windward Islands, Grenada has been fittingly called the Caribbean spice island, for here an array of spices is cultivated for local use and export. While other Caribbean islands also grow spices, Grenada's climate and landscape are suited to production on a larger scale.

The bushy nutmeg tree produces two spices: mace and nutmeg. (Finely powdered nutmeg is often added to rum punch.) Cocoa trees also proliferate in the fertile soil and, during the months of January and February, the hillsides light up with flaming orange flowers which bloom in unison. Clove and cinnamon are locally produced, as is allspice, the dried unripe berry of the pimento tree which itself has hints of cinnamon, cloves and nutmeg. It is sprinkled liberally on meat, added to stews or used to create jerk seasoning.

With the exception of Martinique, the Windward Islands were colonial outposts of Britain, and remain within the British Commonwealth. Martinique, however, has remained in French hands, almost without break, since 1635. The food of the island is widely regarded as some of the best in the Caribbean, combining, as it does, African, Creole and French culinary arts. This marriage of cuisines owes much to the blending of intoxicating spices, fresh seafood and meat, and home-grown tangy fruits. Favourite dishes include chadron, which is sea urchin, and blaff, a dish of freshly poached fish and hot peppers in clear stock.

Saint Lucia's historical battle between the British and French is, thankfully, not played out with its food, which retains its own distinctive quality. Pumpkin soup is served in small eateries, while lobster, flying fish and breadfruit are cooked over hot coals. Pouile dudon – a dish of chicken cooked in coconut and sugar – is a speciality. The food of St Vincent and the Grenadines has a less pronounced character, although it is hearty and simple – made from the fresh fruit and vegetables that grow well in these fertile islands.

Trinidad & Tobago

Trinidad and its tiny neighbour, Tobago, form a single nation and are the most southerly of all the Windward Islands, and the Caribbean islands as a whole. In fact, Trinidad lies close to the coast of Venezuela, to which it was connected just 10,000 years ago.

Christopher Columbus was probably the first European to set foot on the beautiful island of Trinidad, in 1498. The Spanish took control of the island in 1592, and the British captured Trinidad and Tobago from them in 1797, although fierce battles for colonial rights continued between European powers for many years. The British finally relinquished power in 1962, when Trinidad and Tobago gained nationhood. The islands were dubbed the 'Rainbow Country' by Desmond Tutu, in celebration of the nation's diversity. Islanders can trace their roots to places as faraway as Europe, Africa, China, India and the Middle East, a fact that is evident in the full range of Indian, Jamaican, Creole, Chinese and European dishes that are prepared on the islands.

This hotchpotch of people, races, creeds and languages unite at carnival time, when the sound of steel bands resonates through the streets of Trinidad, and its capital, Port-of-Spain, becomes a swirling whirling spectacle of colours, costumes and calypso. It was in Trinidad that calypso developed from the traditional folk songs of African/West Indian immigrants, and these lyrical songs use satire, banter and innuendo to tell the story of the people's hopes and hardships.

While Trinidad is famous for its energy, diversity, vibrancy and bustling business centre, its neighbour Tobago is a more traditional Caribbean island. The lifestyle here is predominantly rural, and a calming wind prevails across the island, encouraging a more leisurely approach to daily chores. Tobago's tranquillity is reflected in a beautiful landscape that has been largely undisturbed by tourism, with interior rainforest and deserted coastal coves and sandy beaches.

Curaçao, Bonaire, Aruba  the Venezuelan Archipelago

A ruba, Bonaire and Curaçao lie in the coastal waters off the Falcon region of Venezuela, and make up three of the six islands of the Netherlands Antilles (St Martin, Saba and St Eustatius are the others).

The islands owe much to a long history of association with the Netherlands, and on Curaçao there are even canals and gabled warehouses which have survived since colonization. Dutch pea soup sits alongside Caribbean fungi (cornmeal and okra balls) and Indian curries. The food of Bonaire, however, is limited by the poor quality of its soil and relative infertility. It is a stark, arid island, visited mostly for its crystal-clear seas and scuba diving, rather than for its cuisine.

On Aruba (pictured left), the people have Dutch, Spanish, French, Portuguese, African, English and East Indian roots. Unsurprisingly, their cuisine is a rich and complex blend of tastes, ingredients and textures. A speciality is rijstaffel – a 'rice table' comprised of many spiced dishes. The original dish was Indonesian, but was developed by Dutch plantation owners, who added more and more variations. Cheeses feature heavily on many menus, and often accompany Dutch-inspired meals that are considered by many to be too heavy for the tropics.

Further east along the Venezuelan coast, lying north of Caracas, are around 50 islands or cays – Los Roques – that are a federal dependency of Venezuela. The string of islands, or archipelago, is formed of coral and has been recognized as a national park since the 1970s. Many tourists visit to enjoy the reefs and wildlife, but only one island, El Gran Roque, is actually inhabited. The cuisine here is a blend of Caribbean, South American and European influences.

Bermuda

Although lying far away from the Caribbean, in the Atlantic Ocean, the islands of Bermuda are an associate member of the Caribbean Community and have noticeable Afro-Caribbean influences in their food. This overseas territory of the United Kingdom is commonly regarded as a single island, but there are some 138 islands in total, forming an extensive coral archipelago.

The land is relatively flat and dry, with no lakes or rivers. Bermuda was first settled in 1609, when shipwrecked sailors from Britain arrived here, on their way to Virginia. Now it supports a booming economy, thanks to a successful financial services sector and tourism. People are drawn to the islands' pink sandy beaches, astonishingly blue seas and subtropical climate.

Most of the islands' food has to be imported; rum, for example, was first brought to the region from the Caribbean in the 1860s. Sweet potatoes and yams, so popular in Caribbean food, also feature in many dishes. The British brought their own culinary delights, including fish soups, or chowders, which are made from a clear fish stock with potatoes and vegetables, and flavoured with rum and sherry. A local condiment, called sherry peppers, is added liberally to provide spice. This unusual mixture is similar to the hot pepper sauces of the American South. It is made from 17 varieties of pepper, steeped in sherry and herbs, and was first used to mask the smell of tainted meat, a problem in the subtropical climate before the advent of refrigeration. Onions grow well on the Bermuda islands, and feature in a range of dishes, including onion soufflé, onion casserole and, of course, onion soup.

Africans were first brought to Bermuda by the British, not as slaves as in other places, but for their expertise in pearl fishing and cultivating West Indian crops. As slavery became more commonplace, however, the relationship between Britons and the Africans in Bermuda became more complex. Afro-Caribbean influences in Bermudan food are seen in rice and bean dishes, black-eyed peas and crab cakes.

Snacks ❧

Soups

❧

Caribbean islanders love to eat on the move, and buying snacks from roadside vendors is a delicious and cheap way to enjoy local cuisine. Since street food is part of the everyday diet of most Caribbean families, it needs to be nutritionally balanced and is often packed with the energy-giving goodness of complex carbohydrates. Fritters are a perennial favourite and satay sticks and sweet potato crisps are perfect appetizers, and easy to prepare at home.

Sweet Potato Crisps with Mango Salsa

Serves 6

For the salsa:

1 large mango, peeled, stoned and cut into small cubes
8 cherry tomatoes, quartered
½ cucumber, peeled if preferred, and finely diced
1 red onion, peeled and finely chopped
pinch sugar
1 red chilli, deseeded and finely chopped
2 tbsp white wine vinegar
2 tbsp olive oil
grated zest and juice of 1 lime
2 tbsp freshly chopped mint

450 g/1 lb sweet potatoes, peeled and thinly sliced
vegetable oil for deep-frying
sea salt

To make the salsa, mix the mango with the tomato, cucumber and onion. Add the sugar, chilli, vinegar, oil and lime zest and juice. Mix together thoroughly, cover with clingfilm and leave for 45–50 minutes.

Soak the sweet potato in cold water for 40 minutes to remove as much of the excess starch as possible. Drain and dry thoroughly on a clean tea towel or absorbent kitchen paper.

Heat the vegetable oil to 190°C/375°F in a deep-fryer. When at the correct temperature, place half the potato in the frying basket, then carefully lower the potato into the hot oil and cook for 4–5 minutes or until golden brown, shaking the basket every minute so that the potato does not stick together.

Drain the potato crisps on absorbent kitchen paper. Spread out in a single layer on a grill tray or baking sheet, sprinkle with sea salt and place under a preheated moderate grill for a few seconds to dry out. Repeat the process with the remaining potato.

Stir the mint into the salsa and serve with the potato crisps.

Mixed Satay Sticks

Serves 4

12 large raw prawns
350 g/12 oz beef rump steak
1 tbsp lime juice
1 garlic clove, peeled and crushed
pinch salt
2 tsp soft dark brown sugar
1 tsp ground allspice
1 tsp ground cinnamon
$1/4$ tsp ground turmeric
1 tbsp vegetable oil
fresh coriander leaves,
to garnish

For the spicy peanut sauce:

1 shallot, peeled and very
finely chopped
1 tsp demerara sugar
50 g/2 oz creamed coconut,
chopped
pinch chilli powder
1 tbsp dark soy sauce
125 g/4 oz crunchy peanut butter

Preheat the grill to high just before required. Soak 8 bamboo skewers in cold water for at least 30 minutes. Peel the prawns, leaving the tails on. Using a sharp knife, remove the black vein along the back of the prawns.

Cut the beef into 1 cm/$1/2$ inch wide strips. Place the prawns and beef in separate bowls, and sprinkle each with $1/2$ tablespoon of the lime juice.

Mix together the garlic, salt, sugar, allspice cinnamon, turmeric and vegetable oil to make a paste. Lightly brush over the prawns and beef. Cover and place in the refrigerator to marinate for at least 30 minutes, but for longer if possible.

Meanwhile, make the sauce. Pour 125 ml/4 fl oz water into a small saucepan, add the shallot and sugar, and heat gently until the sugar has dissolved. Stir in the creamed coconut and chilli powder. When melted, remove from the heat and stir in the soy sauce and peanut butter. Leave to cool slightly, then spoon into a serving dish.

Thread 3 prawns onto each of four skewers and divide the sliced beef between the remaining skewers. Cook the skewers under the preheated grill for 4–5 minutes, turning occasionally. The prawns should be opaque and pink, and the beef browned on the outside, but still pink in the centre. Transfer to warmed individual serving plates, garnish with a few fresh coriander leaves and serve immediately with the warm peanut sauce.

Caribbean Empanadas

Serves 4–6

175 g/6 oz lean fresh beef mince
175 g/6 oz lean fresh pork mince
1 onion, peeled and finely chopped
1 Scotch bonnet chilli, deseeded and finely chopped
1 small red pepper, deseeded and finely chopped
$^1/_2$ tsp ground cloves
1 tsp ground cinnamon
$^1/_2$ tsp ground allspice
1 tsp sugar
1 tbsp tomato purée
6 tbsp water
700 g/1$^1/_2$ lb prepared shortcrust pastry
vegetable oil, for deep-frying
fresh herbs, to garnish
ready-made or shop-bought sweet mango chutney

Place the mince in a nonstick frying pan and cook, stirring, for 5–8 minutes, or until sealed. Break up any lumps with a wooden spoon. Add the onion, chilli and red pepper together with the spices and cook, stirring, for 10 minutes, or until the onion has softened. Sprinkle in the sugar.

Blend the tomato purée with the water and stir into the meat. Bring to the boil, then reduce the heat and simmer gently for 10 minutes. Allow to cool.

Roll the shortcrust pastry out on a lightly floured surface and cut into 10 cm/4 inch rounds. Place a spoonful of the meat mixture onto the centre of each pastry round and brush the edges with water. Fold over, encasing the filling to form small pasties.

Heat the oil to a temperature of 180°C/350°F and deep-fry the empanadas in batches, about three or four at a time, for 3–4 minutes, or until golden. Drain on absorbent kitchen paper. Garnish and serve with the mango chutney.

Rice Cakes with Mango Salsa

Serves 4

225 g/8 oz basmati rice
400 g/14 oz can coconut milk
1 lemon-grass stalk, bruised
1 tbsp finely grated lime zest
1 tbsp vegetable oil,
plus extra for deep-frying
1 garlic clove, peeled and chopped
1 tsp freshly grated root ginger
1 red pepper, deseeded and
finely chopped
1 hot chilli, deseeded and
finely chopped
1 medium egg, beaten
25 g/1 oz dried breadcrumbs

For the salsa:
1 large mango, peeled,
stoned and finely chopped
1 small red onion,
peeled and finely chopped
2 tbsp freshly chopped coriander
2 tbsp freshly chopped basil
1 hot chilli, deseeded and sliced
juice of 1 lime

Wash the rice in several changes of water until the water stays relatively clear. Drain, place in a saucepan with a tight-fitting lid and add the coconut milk, lemon grass and lime zest. Bring to the boil, cover and cook over the lowest possible heat for 10 minutes. Turn off the heat and leave to stand for 10 minutes, without lifting the lid.

Heat the wok, then add the 1 tablespoon oil and, when hot, add the garlic, ginger, red pepper and chilli. Stir-fry for 1–2 minutes until just softened, then place in a large bowl.

When the rice is ready, turn into the mixing bowl and add the egg. Season to taste with salt and pepper and mix together well. Put the breadcrumbs into a shallow dish. Form the rice mixture into eight cakes and coat them in the breadcrumbs. Chill the rice cakes in the refrigerator for 30 minutes.

Meanwhile, make the mango salsa by mixing together all the salsa ingredients in a bowl. Reserve.

Fill a clean wok about one-third full of vegetable oil. Heat to 190°C/375°F, or until a cube of bread browns in 30 seconds. Cook the rice cakes, one or two at a time, for 2–3 minutes until golden and crisp. Drain on absorbent kitchen paper. Serve with the mango salsa.

Cassava Chips

Serves 4

450 g/1 lb cassava
$^1/_2$ tsp salt
600 ml/1 pt vegetable oil,
for deep-frying
sea salt and freshly ground black
pepper or 1 tsp jerk seasoning
2 tbsp finely shredded coconut

Peel the cassava and cut into thick chips about 2.5 cm/1 inch thick.
Leave the chips in cold water while preparing the rest of the
cassava to prevent discoloration.

Drain the cassava chips and place in a large saucepan with the
$^1/_2$ teaspoon salt. Cover with cold water and bring to the boil.
Reduce the heat to a simmer, cover with a lid and cook for 20–25
minutes, or until just tender. Drain, pat dry and reserve.

Heat the oil in a deep-fryer to a temperature of 190˚C/375˚F.
Meanwhile, have ready some kitchen paper, the sea salt and ground
black pepper (or the jerk seasoning), and the shredded coconut.

When the oil has reached the correct temperature, place a layer of
cassava chips in the frying basket and lower into the hot oil. Cook
for 5 minutes, or until crisp and golden. Drain on kitchen paper and
sprinkle with either the salt and pepper or the jerk seasoning.
Sprinkle with the coconut. Repeat until all the chips are cooked.
Serve warm.

Plantain Appetizer

Serves 4

2 green plantains
3 tbsp vegetable oil
1 small onion, very thinly sliced
1 yellow plantain
$1/2$ garlic clove, crushed
cayenne pepper, for sprinkling
salt, for sprinkling

Peel one of the green plantains and cut into wafer-thin rounds, preferably using a swivel-headed potato peeler.

Heat 1 tablespoon of the oil in a large frying pan and fry the plantain slices for 2–3 minutes until golden, turning occasionally. Transfer to a plate lined with kitchen paper and keep warm.

Coarsely grate the other green plantain and mix with the onion.

Heat 1 tablespoon of the remaining oil in the pan and fry the plantain and onion mixture for 2–3 minutes until golden, turning occasionally. Transfer to the plate with the plantain slices.

Peel the yellow plantain and cut into small chunks. Sprinkle with cayenne pepper. Heat the remaining oil and fry the yellow plantain and garlic for 4–5 minutes until brown. Drain and sprinkle with salt.

Arrange all the plantain mixtures in a large warm serving dish and serve immediately.

Corn Fritters with Hot Spicy Relish

Makes 16–20

For the spicy relish:

3 tbsp vegetable oil
1 onion, peeled and very
finely chopped
¹/₄ tsp dried crushed chillies
2 garlic cloves, peeled and crushed
2 tbsp lime juice

325 g/11 oz can sweetcorn kernels,
drained
1 onion, peeled and very
finely chopped
1 spring onion, trimmed and very
finely chopped
¹/₂ tsp hot chilli powder
1 tsp ground allspice
4 tbsp plain flour
1 tsp baking powder
1 medium egg
300 ml/10 fl oz vegetable oil
salt and freshly ground black pepper
fresh coriander sprigs, to garnish

First make the relish. Heat a wok, add the vegetable oil and, when hot, add the onion and stir-fry for 3–4 minutes, or until softened. Add the chilli and garlic, stir-fry for 1 minute, then leave to cool slightly. Stir in the lime juice, transfer to a food processor and blend until the consistency of chutney. Reserve.

Put the sweetcorn in a food processor and blend briefly until just mashed. Transfer to a bowl with the onions, chilli powder, allspice, flour, baking powder and egg. Season to taste with salt and pepper, and mix together to form a batter.

Heat a wok, add the oil and heat to 180°C/350°F. Working in batches, drop a few spoonfuls of the sweetcorn batter into the oil and deep-fry for 3–4 minutes, until golden and crispy, turning occasionally. Using a slotted spoon, remove the fritters and drain on absorbent kitchen paper. Arrange on a warmed serving platter, garnish with the fresh coriander sprigs and serve immediately, accompanied by the relish.

Cream of Pumpkin Soup

Serves 4

900 g/2 lb pumpkin flesh (after
peeling and discarding
the seeds)
4 tbsp olive oil
1 large onion, peeled and
finely chopped
1 leek, trimmed and finely chopped
1 carrot, peeled and cut into
small dice
2 celery stalks, cut into small dice
4 garlic cloves, peeled and crushed
1 habañero chilli,
deseeded and finely chopped
1 tsp ground allspice
$\frac{1}{4}$ tsp freshly grated nutmeg
150 ml/5 fl oz pint coconut milk
$\frac{1}{4}$ tsp cayenne pepper
salt and freshly ground
black pepper
warm herby bread, to serve

Cut the pumpkin flesh into 2.5 cm/1 inch cubes. Heat the olive oil in a large saucepan and cook the pumpkin for 2–3 minutes, coating it completely with the oil.

Add the onion, leek, carrot and celery to the saucepan with the garlic and chilli. Cook, stirring, for 5 minutes, or until the vegetables have begun to soften. Cover the vegetables with 1.7 litres/3 pints water and bring to the boil. Season with plenty of salt and pepper, the allspice and nutmeg. Cover and simmer for 15–20 minutes or until all the vegetables are tender.

Remove from the heat, cool slightly, then pour into a food processor or blender. Liquidize to form a smooth purée, then pass through a sieve into a clean saucepan.

Adjust the seasoning to taste and add all but 2 tablespoons of the coconut milk and enough water to obtain a thick and creamy consistency. Bring the soup to boiling point, add the cayenne pepper and serve immediately swirled with the remaining coconut milk and accompanied by warm herby bread.

Sweet Potato Cakes with Mango Tomato Salsa

Serves 4

700 g/1½ lb sweet potatoes,
peeled and cut into large chunks
25 g/1 oz butter
1 onion, peeled and chopped
1 garlic clove, peeled and crushed
pinch freshly grated nutmeg
1 tsp ground allspice
1 medium egg, beaten
50 g/2 oz quick-cook polenta
2 tbsp vegetable oil
salt and freshly ground black pepper
salad leaves, to serve

For the salsa:

1 ripe mango, peeled, stoned
and diced
6 cherry tomatoes, cut into wedges
4 spring onions, trimmed and
thinly sliced
1 hot chilli, deseeded and
finely chopped
finely grated zest and juice of ½ lime
2 tbsp freshly chopped mint
1 tsp clear honey

Steam or cook the sweet potato in lightly salted boiling water for 15–20 minutes until tender. Drain well, then mash until smooth.

Melt the butter in a saucepan. Add the onion and garlic, and cook gently for 10 minutes until soft. Add to the mashed sweet potato and season with the nutmeg, allspice, salt and pepper. Stir together until mixed thoroughly. Leave to cool.

Shape the mixture into four oval potato cakes, about 2.5 cm/1 inch thick. Dip first in the beaten egg, allowing the excess to fall back into the bowl, then coat in the polenta. Refrigerate for at least 30 minutes.

Meanwhile, mix together all the ingredients for the salsa. Spoon into a serving bowl, cover with clingfilm and leave to sit at room temperature to allow the flavours to develop.

Heat the oil in a frying pan and cook the potato cakes for 4–5 minutes on each side. Serve with the salsa and salad leaves.

Rice and

Curry

Curried dishes have long been Caribbean favourites, reflecting the islands' history of colonization and immigration. When Indians brought their hot spices and fragrant curry powders, they received an enthusiastic welcome, not least by the British contingent, who had developed a craving for curry in India. Like curries, rice dishes are ubiquitous in the region, and jambalaya (a Creole dish of rice with seafood, ham or chicken, with herbs and spices) is a versatile and popular dish.

Rice Papaya Salad

Serves 4

175 g/6 oz easy-cook basmati rice
1 cinnamon stick, bruised
zest and juice of 2 limes
zest and juice of 2 lemons
1 habañero chilli, deseeded and
finely chopped
1–2 tbsp hot pepper sauce
1 tbsp soft light brown sugar
1 papaya, peeled and
seeds removed
1 mango, peeled and
stone removed
1 green chilli, deseeded
and finely chopped
2 tbsp freshly chopped coriander
1 tbsp freshly chopped mint
250 g/9 oz cooked chicken
50 g/2 oz roasted peanuts, chopped
strips of pitta bread, to serve

Rinse and drain the rice, and pour into a saucepan. Add the cinnamon stick and 450 ml/15 fl oz pint boiling salted water. Bring to the boil, reduce the heat to very low, cover and cook without stirring for 15–18 minutes, or until all the liquid is absorbed. The rice should be light and fluffy, and have steam holes on the surface. Remove the cinnamon stick and stir in the zest from 1 lime.

To make the dressing, put the remaining zest, lime and lemon juice, habañero chilli, hot pepper sauce and sugar in a food processor. Mix for a few minutes until blended. Alternatively, place all these ingredients in a screw-top jar and shake until well blended. Pour half the dressing over the hot rice and toss until the rice glistens.

Slice the papaya and mango into thin slices, then place in a bowl. Add the chopped green chilli, coriander and mint. Place the chicken on a chopping board, then remove and discard any skin or sinew. Cut into fine shreds and add to the bowl with the peanuts.

Add the remaining dressing to the chicken mixture and stir until all the ingredients are lightly coated. Spoon the rice onto a platter, pile the chicken mixture on top and serve with warm strips of pitta bread.

Creole Jambalaya

Serves 6–8

For the seasoning mix:
2 dried bay leaves; 1 tsp salt;
2 tsp cayenne pepper, or to taste;
2 tsp dried thyme; 1 tsp each ground
white and black pepper, or to taste

3 tbsp vegetable oil
125 g/4 oz ham
225 g/8 oz smoked pork sausage,
cut into chunks
2 large onions, peeled and chopped
4 celery sticks, trimmed and chopped
2 green peppers, deseeded and chopped
2 garlic cloves, peeled and finely chopped
350 g/12 oz skinless
chicken breast fillets, diced
400 g/ 14 oz can chopped tomatoes
600 ml/1 pint fish stock
400 g/14 oz long-grain white rice
4 spring onions, trimmed and
coarsely chopped
275 g/10 oz raw prawns,
peeled and deveined
250 g/9 oz white crab meat

Mix all the seasoning ingredients together in a small bowl and reserve.

Heat 2 tablespoons of the oil in a large flameproof casserole over a medium heat. Add the ham and sausage, and cook, stirring often, for 7–8 minutes until golden. Remove from the pan and reserve.

Add the remaining oil, onion, celery and peppers to the casserole and cook for about 4 minutes or until softened, stirring occasionally. Stir in the garlic, then, using a slotted spoon, transfer all the vegetables to a plate and reserve with the ham and sausage.

Add the chicken to the casserole and cook for about 4 minutes or until beginning to colour, turning once. Stir in the seasoning mix and turn the chicken pieces to coat well. Return the ham, sausage and vegetables to the casserole and stir well. Add the chopped tomatoes (with their juice, and the stock), and bring to the boil.

Stir in the rice and reduce the heat to low. Cover and simmer for 12 minutes. Uncover, stir in the spring onion and prawns, and cook, covered, for a further 4 minutes. Add the crab and gently stir in. Cook for 2–3 minutes, or until the rice is tender. Remove from the heat, cover and leave to stand for 5 minutes before serving (after having removed the bay leaves).

Jambalayan-style Fried Rice

Serves 6

450 g/1 lb long-grain rice
900 ml/1¹/₂ pints hot chicken or fish stock
2 fresh bay leaves
2 tbsp vegetable oil
2 medium onions, peeled and
roughly chopped
1 green pepper, deseeded and
roughly chopped
2 celery stalks, trimmed and
roughly chopped
3 garlic cloves, peeled and finely chopped
1 tsp dried oregano
300 g/11 oz skinless
chicken breast fillets, chopped
125 g/4 oz chorizo sausage, chopped
3 tomatoes, peeled and chopped
12 large raw prawns, peeled and
deveined if preferred
hot pepper sauce, to taste
4 spring onions, trimmed and
finely chopped
2 tbsp freshly chopped parsley
salt and freshly ground black pepper

Put the rice, stock and bay leaves into a large saucepan and bring to the boil. Cover with a tight-fitting lid and simmer for 10 minutes over a very low heat. Remove from the heat and leave for a further 10 minutes.

Meanwhile, heat a large wok, then add the oil and heat. When hot, add the onion, green pepper, celery, garlic and oregano. Stir-fry for 6 minutes, or until all the vegetables have softened. Add the chicken and chorizo, and stir-fry for a further 6 minutes, or until lightly browned.

Add the tomato and cook over a medium heat for 2–3 minutes until collapsed. Stir in the prawns and hot pepper sauce and cook for a further 4 minutes, or until the prawns are cooked through. Stir in the cooked rice, spring onion and parsley, and season to taste with salt and pepper. Serve immediately.

Calypso Rice with Curried Bananas

Serves 4

2 tbsp vegetable oil

1 medium onion, peeled and
finely chopped

1 garlic clove, peeled and crushed

1 habañero chilli, deseeded and
finely chopped

1 red pepper, deseeded and
finely chopped

225 g/8 oz basmati rice

juice of 1 lime

350 ml/12 fl oz vegetable stock

200 g/7 oz can black-eyed beans,
drained and rinsed

2 tbsp freshly chopped parsley

salt and freshly ground black pepper

fresh coriander sprigs, to garnish

For the curried bananas:

4 green bananas

2 tbsp vegetable oil

2 tsp mild curry paste

200 ml/7 fl oz coconut milk

Heat the oil in a large frying pan and gently cook the onion for 10 minutes until soft. Add the garlic, chilli and red pepper, and cook for 2–3 minutes.

Rinse the rice under cold running water, then add to the pan and stir. Pour in the lime juice and stock, bring to the boil, cover and simmer for 12–15 minutes, or until the rice is tender and the stock is absorbed.

Stir in the black-eyed beans and parsley, and season to taste with salt and pepper. Leave to stand, covered, for 5 minutes before serving, to allow the beans to warm through.

While the rice is cooking, make the curried green bananas. Remove the skins from the bananas – they may need to be cut off with a sharp knife. Slice the flesh thickly. Heat the oil in a frying pan and cook the bananas, in 2 batches, for 2–3 minutes, or until lightly browned.

Pour the coconut milk into the pan and stir in the curry paste. Add the banana slices to the coconut milk and simmer, uncovered, over a low heat for 8–10 minutes, or until the bananas are very soft and the coconut milk slightly reduced.

Spoon the rice onto warmed serving plates, garnish with coriander and serve immediately with the curried bananas.

Spicy Mahi Mahi Rice

Serves 4

1 tbsp plain flour
1 tbsp freshly chopped coriander
1 tsp ground allspice
1 tsp chilli powder
550 g/1¼ lb thick-cut mahi mahi fillet
(or cod), skinned and cut into
large chunks
4 tbsp vegetable oil
50 g/2 oz cashew nuts
1 bunch of spring onions,
trimmed and diagonally sliced
1 habañero chilli,
deseeded and chopped
1 carrot, peeled and
cut into matchsticks
125 g/4 oz frozen peas
450 g/1 lb cooked long-grain rice
2 tbsp hot pepper sauce
2 tbsp soy sauce

Mix together the flour, coriander, allspice and chilli powder on a large plate. Coat the fish in the spice mixture, then place on a baking sheet, cover and chill in the refrigerator for 30 minutes.

Heat a large wok, then add 2 tablespoons of the oil and heat until almost smoking. Stir-fry the cashew nuts for 1 minute until browned, then remove and reserve.

Add a further 1 tablespoon of the oil and heat until almost smoking. Add the fish and stir-fry for 2 minutes. Using a fish slice, turn the fish pieces over and cook for a further 2 minutes until golden. Remove from the wok, place on a warm plate, cover and keep warm.

Add the remaining oil to the wok, heat until almost smoking, then stir-fry the spring onions and chilli for 1 minute before adding the carrot and peas, and stir-frying for a further 2 minutes. Stir in the rice, hot pepper sauce, soy sauce and reserved cashew nuts, and stir-fry for 3 more minutes. Add the fish, heat for 1 minute, then serve immediately.

Nutty Fruit Pilaf

Serves 4–6

50 g/2 oz butter
6 cracked green cardamom pods
1 cinnamon stick, bruised
2 bay leaves
450 g/1 lb basmati rice
600 ml/1 pint chicken stock
1 onion, peeled and finely chopped
50 g/2 oz flaked almonds
50 g/2 oz shelled pistachios,
roughly chopped
125 g/4 oz ready-to-eat dried
mangoes, roughly chopped
50 g/2 oz ready-to-eat dried papaya,
roughly chopped
30 g/1 oz dried figs
275 g/10 oz skinless
chicken breast fillets,
cut into chunks
dash Tabasco sauce
salt and freshly ground black pepper
fresh parsley or coriander leaves,
to garnish

Melt half the butter in a saucepan or casserole dish with a tight-fitting lid. Add the cardamom pods and cinnamon stick, and cook for about 30 seconds before adding the bay leaves and rice. Stir well to coat the rice in the butter and add the stock. Bring to the boil, cover tightly and cook very gently for 15 minutes. Remove from the heat and leave to stand for a further 5 minutes.

Melt the remaining butter in a wok and, when foaming, add the onion, flaked almonds and pistachios. Stir-fry for 3–4 minutes until the nuts are beginning to brown. Remove and reserve.

Reduce the heat slightly and add the dried mango, papaya, figs and chicken, and continue stir-frying for a further 7–8 minutes until the chicken is cooked through. Return the nuts to the mixture and toss to mix.

Remove from the heat, then remove the cinnamon stick and bay leaves from the rice. Add the cooked rice to the chicken mixture and stir together well to mix. Season to taste with Tabasco sauce, salt and black pepper. Garnish with fresh parsley or coriander leaves, and serve immediately.

Caribbean Goat Curry

Serves 4

675 g/1 lb 8 oz boneless kid or
goat meat
1–2 tsp curry powder
2.5 cm/1 inch piece of fresh root
ginger, peeled and grated
2 tsp ground turmeric
1 tsp ground allspice
few sprigs fresh thyme,
leaves picked
2 fresh bay leaves
2 tbsp vegetable oil
1 medium onion,
peeled and chopped
2 or 3 garlic cloves,
peeled and chopped
1 habañero chilli,
deseeded and chopped
1 tbsp tomato purée
600 ml/1 pt lamb stock
1 tbsp freshly chopped
coriander sprigs, to garnish
salt and freshly ground black pepper
freshly prepared rice and salad, to serve

Cut the meat into small cubes, discarding any fat or gristle. Place the meat in a bowl and sprinkle over the curry powder and ginger, together with the other spices. Add half the thyme and one of the bay leaves. Leave to marinate in the refrigerator for at least 4 hours, preferably overnight.

Heat the oil in a large heavy-based saucepan over a medium high heat. Remove the meat from the spice marinade, reserving any remaining marinade. Sauté the meat until sealed all over. Remove from the pan with a slotted spoon and reserve. Add the onion, garlic and chilli to the oil remaining in the pan and sauté for 5 minutes, stirring frequently. Return the meat to the pan together with the reserved marinade. Cook, stirring, for 3 minutes.

Blend the tomato purée with the stock and add to the pan together with a little salt and pepper and the remaining thyme and bay leaf. Bring to the boil, then reduce the heat to a simmer and cover with a lid.

Cook over a gentle heat for 1^1/$_2$ hours, or until the meat is very tender. Adjust seasoning if necessary, and stir in the chopped coriander. Remove the bay leaves. Serve garnished with the coriander sprigs accompanied by the freshly cooked rice and salad.

Curried Fish Caribbean Style

Serves 4–6

4 fish steaks, such as cod, salmon
or tuna, each about 150 g/5 oz
in weight
freshly milled rock salt, to sprinkle
4 tbsp lime juice
2 tbsp groundnut oil
3 garlic cloves, peeled and chopped
1 onion, peeled and chopped
225 g/8 oz tomatoes,
peeled and chopped
1 tsp turmeric
$^1/_2$ tsp chilli powder, or to taste
1 tsp ground allspice
1 tsp dried thyme
1 tsp dried oregano
1 tbsp freshly chopped coriander
1–3 tsp hot pepper sauce, to taste
150 ml/$^1/_4$ pint water
4 spring onions, trimmed and chopped,
to garnish (optional)
freshly cooked vegetables, to serve

Preheat the oven to 180˚C/350˚F/Gas Mark 4. Lightly rinse the fish fillets and place in a lightly oiled shallow ovenproof dish. Sprinkle with a little salt and drizzle over the lime juice. Cover and leave in the refrigerator for 10 minutes while making the sauce.

Heat the groundnut oil in a saucepan, add the garlic and onion and fry for 3 minutes. Add the tomatoes, spices, herbs, hot pepper sauce, to taste, and the water. Bring to the boil, then reduce the heat and simmer, stirring, for 10 minutes, or until slightly reduced.

Spoon the sauce over the fish fillets, cover with foil and cook in the preheated oven for 15 minutes. Remove the foil and cook for a further 5 minutes, or until the fish is tender. Sprinkle with spring onions (if using), and serve on warmed plates with freshly cooked vegetables.

Coconut Fish Curry

Serves 4

2 tbsp vegetable oil
1 medium onion, peeled and very
finely chopped
1 yellow pepper, deseeded and
finely chopped
1 garlic clove, peeled and crushed
1 tbsp hot curry paste
2.5 cm/1 inch piece of root ginger,
peeled and grated
1 habañero chilli, deseeded and
finely chopped
400 ml/14 oz can coconut milk
700 g/1^1/$_2$ lb firm white fish,
e.g. monkfish fillets, skinned and
cut into chunks
225 g/8 oz basmati rice
1 tbsp freshly chopped coriander,
plus extra sprigs to garnish
1 tbsp mango chutney
salt and freshly ground
black pepper
lime wedges, to serve
Greek-style yogurt, to serve
warm naan bread, to serve

Put 1 tablespoon of the oil into a large frying pan and, when hot, cook the onion, pepper and garlic for 5 minutes, or until soft. Add the remaining oil, curry paste, ginger and chilli, and cook for a further minute.

Pour in the coconut milk and bring to the boil. Reduce the heat and simmer gently for 5 minutes, stirring occasionally. Add the monkfish to the pan and continue to simmer gently for 5–10 minutes, or until the fish is tender, but not overcooked.

Meanwhile, cook the rice in a saucepan of boiling salted water for 15 minutes, or until tender. Drain the rice thoroughly and turn out into a serving dish.

Stir the chopped coriander and chutney gently into the fish curry, and season to taste with salt and pepper. Spoon the fish curry over the cooked rice, garnish with lime wedges and extra coriander sprigs, and serve immediately with spoonfuls of Greek yogurt and warm naan bread.

Salmon Mango Curry

Serves 4–6

4 salmon fillets, each about
150 g/5 oz in weight
2 tbsp vegetable oil
$^{1}/_{2}$–1 yellow Scotch bonnet chilli,
deseeded and chopped
4 garlic cloves, peeled and chopped
2 medium onions,
peeled and chopped
1$^{1}/_{2}$ tsp ground allspice
1 tsp ground cloves
1 tsp ground cinnamon stick
1 tsp demerara sugar
400 g/14 oz can chopped tomatoes
2 tbsp ready-made or bought
mango chutney
1 large fresh ripe mango
1 tsp hot pepper sauce, or to taste
2 tbsp freshly chopped
flat-leaf parsley
freshly cooked white and wild rice,
to serve

Lightly rinse the salmon fillets and discard any pin bones, if necessary. Place in a shallow dish and reserve.

Heat the oil in a frying pan, add the chilli, garlic and onions and fry for 3 minutes. Add the spices and cook, stirring, for 2 minutes. Remove from the heat, cool slightly, then remove half the spice mixture and use to spread over the top of the salmon. Cover lightly and leave in the refrigerator for 15 minutes.

Add the sugar and tomatoes to the spices remaining in the pan. Half-fill the empty tomato can with water, swirl to remove any remaining pieces of tomato and add to the pan.

Bring the sauce to the boil, then reduce the heat, cover and simmer for 5–7 minutes, or until cooked, stirring occasionally. Carefully add the fillets to the frying pan. Stir in the chutney. Bring to the boil, then reduce the heat and simmer gently for 5 minutes.

Meanwhile, peel the mango and discard the stone. Chop the flesh and add to the pan. Add hot pepper sauce to taste and continue to simmer for 3–5 minutes, or until the fish is tender. Sprinkle with chopped parsley and serve with cooked rice.

Aromatic Chicken Curry

Serves 4

2 tsp allspice
1 tbsp ground cinnamon
2 tsp hot curry paste
125 g/4 oz red lentils,
rinsed thoroughly and drained
1 bay leaf
small strip of lemon zest
600 ml/1 pint chicken or
vegetable stock
Tabasco sauce, to taste
8 chicken thighs, skinned
175 g/6 oz spinach leaves,
rinsed and shredded
1 tbsp freshly
chopped coriander
2 tsp lemon juice
salt and freshly ground
black pepper
freshly cooked rice, to serve
lemon wedges, to serve
plain natural yogurt, to serve

Dry-roast the allspice and cinnamon in a large saucepan over a low heat for about 30 seconds. Stir in the curry paste.

Add the lentils to the saucepan with the bay leaf and lemon zest, then pour in the stock and add the Tabasco sauce. Stir, then slowly bring to the boil. Turn down the heat, half-cover the saucepan with a lid and simmer gently for 5 minutes, stirring occasionally.

Secure the chicken thighs with cocktail sticks to keep their shape. Place in the saucepan and half-cover. Simmer for 15 minutes.

Stir in the shredded spinach and cook for a further 25 minutes, or until the chicken is very tender and the sauce is thick. Remove the bay leaf and lemon zest. Stir in the coriander and lemon juice, then season to taste with salt and pepper. Serve immediately with the rice, lemon wedges and a little natural yogurt.

Creole Chicken Curry

Serves 4–6

8 garlic cloves, peeled and
cut in half
¹/₂ tsp salt
1 tbsp grated lime or lemon zest
1 tbsp fresh thyme leaves
1 tbsp fresh oregano leaves
2 tsp freshly chopped coriander
4 chicken thighs
2 tbsp vegetable oil
1 tbsp curry paste
1 tbsp tamarind paste
1 tbsp Worcestershire sauce
2 tsp demerara sugar
350 g/12 oz sweet potatoes, peeled
and cut into small chunks
250 ml/8 fl oz orange or mango juice
150 ml/¹/₄ pint chicken stock
few curry leaves
100 g/4 oz sugar snap peas
2 tbsp freshly chopped coriander,
to garnish

Preheat the oven to 190°C/375°F/Gas Mark 5. Place half the garlic in a food processor with the salt, citrus zest and fresh herbs and blend to form a paste.

Skin the chicken portions, if preferred, and make small incisions into the flesh. Insert the remaining garlic into the incisions and spread with the prepared herb paste. Place on a plate, cover lightly and leave to marinate in the refrigerator for at least 30 minutes.

When ready to cook, heat the oil in a frying pan, add the chicken and brown on all sides. Remove and place in an ovenproof casserole dish. Add the curry paste with the tamarind paste, Worcestershire sauce and sugar and cook, stirring, for 2 minutes. Add the sweet potato chunks with the juice and stock and bring to the boil. Boil gently, stirring, for 2 minutes, add the curry leaves then pour over the chicken.

Cover with a lid and cook in the preheated oven for 30 minutes. Add the sugar snaps and cook for a further 5–8 minutes, or until the chicken is thoroughly cooked. Serve sprinkled with chopped coriander.

Pumpkin Chickpea Curry

Serves 4

1 tbsp vegetable oil
1 small onion, peeled and sliced
2 garlic cloves, peeled and
finely chopped
2.5 cm/1 inch piece root ginger,
peeled and grated
1 tsp ground allspice
$^1/_2$ tsp ground cloves
$^1/_2$ tsp ground turmeric
1 tsp ground cinnamon
2 tomatoes, chopped
2 habañero chillies, deseeded and
finely chopped
450 g/1 lb pumpkin or butternut
squash flesh, cubed
1 tbsp hot curry paste
300 ml/10 fl oz pint vegetable stock
1 large firm banana
400 g/14 oz can chickpeas,
drained and rinsed
salt and freshly ground black pepper
1 tbsp freshly chopped coriander,
plus extra sprigs, to garnish
rice or flat bread, to serve

Heat the oil in a saucepan and add the onion. Fry gently for 5 minutes until softened. Add the garlic, ginger and spices, and fry for a further minute. Add the tomato and chilli, and cook for another minute.

Next add the pumpkin and curry paste, and fry gently for 3–4 minutes before adding the stock. Stir well, bring to the boil and simmer for 20 minutes until the pumpkin is tender.

Thickly slice the banana and add to the pumpkin along with the chickpeas. Simmer for a further 5 minutes. Season to taste with salt and pepper, and add the chopped coriander. Serve immediately, garnished with the extra coriander sprigs and accompanied by rice or flat bread.

Lobster Prawn Curry

Serves 4

225 g/8 oz cooked lobster meat, shelled if necessary
225 g/8 oz raw tiger prawns, peeled and deveined
2 tbsp vegetable oil
2 bunches spring onions, trimmed and thickly sliced
2 garlic cloves, peeled and chopped
2.5 cm/1 inch piece fresh root ginger, peeled and cut into matchsticks
2 tbsp hot curry paste
200 ml/7 fl oz coconut milk
grated zest and juice of 1 lime
3 tbsp freshly chopped coriander
salt and freshly ground black pepper
freshly cooked rice, to serve
lemon wedges, to serve

Using a sharp knife, slice the lobster meat thickly. Wash the tiger prawns and pat dry with absorbent kitchen paper. Make a small 1 cm/^{1}/$_2$ inch cut at the tail end of each prawn.

Heat a large wok, then add the oil and, when hot, stir-fry the lobster and tiger prawns for 4–6 minutes, or until pink. Using a slotted spoon, transfer to a plate and keep warm in a low oven.

Add the spring onion and stir-fry for 2 minutes, then stir in the garlic and ginger. Stir-fry for a further 2 minutes. Add the curry paste and stir-fry for another minute.

Pour in the coconut milk, lime zest and juice. Season to taste with salt and pepper. Bring to the boil and simmer for 1 minute. Return the prawns, lobster and any juices to the wok and simmer for 2 minutes. Stir in two thirds of the freshly chopped coriander, garnished with the remaining coriander and accompanied by freshly cooked rice. Serve immediately.

Fish and Seafood

It is no wonder that the islands of the Caribbean, buffeted as they are by the waves of the Atlantic Ocean and Caribbean Sea, are home to a range of seafood dishes. Most of the fish in the region are small reef fish, however, which cannot be caught in large enough numbers, so some fish has to be imported. Even the ubiquitous red snapper has been overfished to such an extent that other similar species are now sometimes substituted in traditional recipes.

Gingered Cod Steaks

Serves 4

4 spring onions, trimmed and cut
into thin strips
2.5 cm/1 inch piece fresh root ginger,
peeled and coarsely grated
2 tsp freshly chopped parsley
1 tbsp soft brown sugar
4 x 175 g /6 oz thick cod steaks
25 g/1 oz butter cut into small cubes
salt and freshly ground
black pepper
hot pepper sauce, to serve
freshly cooked vegetables,
to serve

Preheat the grill to a medium heat and line the grill rack with a layer of foil. Coarsely grate the piece of ginger. Mix the spring onion, ginger, parsley and sugar. Add 1 tablespoon water.

Pat the fish steaks dry with kitchen towel. Season to taste with salt and pepper. Place on four separate 20.5 x 20.5 cm/ 8 x 8 inch foil squares. Carefully spoon the spring onion mixture over the fish. Dot the butter place over the fish. Loosely fold the foil over the steaks to enclose the fish and to make a parcel.

Place the parcels under the preheated grill and cook for 10–12 minutes, or until the fish is cooked and the flesh has turned opaque. Place the fish parcels on individual serving plates. Serve immediately with the fresh vegetables.

Barbecued Fish Kebabs

Serves 4

For the sauce:

150 ml/5 fl oz pint fish stock
5 tbsp tomato ketchup
2 tbsp Worcestershire sauce
2 tbsp wine vinegar
2 tbsp soft brown sugar
2 drops hot pepper sauce
2 tbsp tomato purée
450 g/1 lb herring or
mackerel fillets, cut into chunks
2 small red onions,
peeled and quartered
16 cherry tomatoes
salt and freshly ground
black pepper

If using wooden skewers, soak in cold water for 30 minutes to prevent them from catching alight during cooking.

Meanwhile, prepare the sauce. Put the fish stock, tomato ketchup, Worcestershire sauce, vinegar, sugar, Tabasco and tomato purée in a small saucepan. Stir well and leave to simmer for 5 minutes.

When ready to cook the kebabs, line a grill rack with a single layer of foil and heat the grill to high. Drain the skewers, if necessary, then thread the fish chunks, quartered red onions and cherry tomatoes alternately on to the skewers. Season the kebabs to taste with salt and pepper, and brush with the sauce.

Grill under the hot grill for 8–10 minutes, basting with the sauce occasionally during cooking. Turn the kebabs often to ensure that they are cooked thoroughly and evenly on all sides. Serve immediately with couscous.

Hot Salsa-filled Sole

Serves 4

For the salsa:

1 small mango peeled, stoned and
finely chopped
8 cherry tomatoes, quartered
1 small red onion, peeled and
finely chopped
pinch sugar
1 red chilli, deseeded, stoned and
finely chopped
2 tbsp white wine vinegar
zest and juice of 1 lime
1 tbsp olive oil
sea salt and freshly ground
black pepper
8 x 175 g/6 oz lemon
sole fillets, skinned
150 ml/5 fl oz pint orange juice
2 tbsp lemon juice
2 tbsp freshly chopped mint
lime wedges, to garnish
salad leaves, to serve

First make the salsa. Put all the salsa ingredients in a small bowl. Season to taste with salt and pepper. Mix thoroughly and let stand for 30 minutes to allow the flavours to develop.

Lay the fish fillets on a board skin-side up and pile the salsa on the tail end of the fillets. Fold the fillets in half, season and place in a large shallow frying pan. Pour over the orange and lemon juice.

Bring to a gentle boil, then reduce the heat to a simmer. Cover and cook over a low heat for 7–10 minutes, adding a little water if the liquid is evaporating. Remove the cover, add the mint and cook uncovered for a further 3 minutes. Garnish with the lime wedges and serve immediately with the salad leaves.

Tuna Chowder

Serves 4

2 tsp vegetable oil
1 onion, peeled and finely chopped
2 celery sticks, trimmed and
finely sliced
300 g/10 oz fresh tuna steak,
cut into small pieces
1 tbsp plain flour
600 ml/1 pint semi-skimmed milk
320 g/11 oz can sweetcorn in
water, drained
2 tsp freshly chopped thyme
pinch cayenne pepper
2 tbsp freshly chopped parsley
salt and freshly ground
black pepper

Heat the oil in a large heavy-based saucepan. Add the onion and celery, and gently cook for about 5 minutes, stirring from time to time until the onion is softened. Next stir in the tuna and cook for 2 minutes. Stir in the flour and cook for about 1 minute to thicken.

Draw the pan off the heat and gradually pour in the milk, stirring throughout. Add the drained sweetcorn and the thyme. Mix gently, then bring to the boil. Cover and simmer for 5 minutes.

Remove the pan from the heat and season to taste with salt and pepper. Sprinkle the chowder with the cayenne pepper and chopped parsley. Divide into soup bowls and serve immediately.

Sweetcorn Crab Soup

Serves 4

450 g/1 lb fresh corn on the cob
1.3 litres/2^{1}/4 pints chicken stock
2 or 3 spring onions,
trimmed and finely chopped
1 cm/^{1}/2 inch piece fresh root
ginger, peeled and finely chopped
1 tbsp rum
2–3 tsp soy sauce
1 tsp soft light brown sugar
2 tsp cornflour
225 g/8 oz white crab meat,
fresh or canned
1 medium egg white
1 tsp chilli-flavoured oil
1–2 tbsp freshly chopped coriander
salt and freshly ground black pepper

Rinse the corn cobs and pat dry with absorbent kitchen paper. Using a sharp knife and holding the corn cobs at an angle to the cutting board, cut down along the cobs to remove the kernels, then scrape the cobs to remove any excess milky residue. Put the kernels and the milky residue into a large wok.

Add the chicken stock to the wok and place over a high heat. Bring to the boil, stirring and pressing some of the kernels against the side of the wok to squeeze out the starch to help thicken the soup. Simmer for 15 minutes, stirring occasionally.

Add the spring onion, ginger, rum, soy sauce and brown sugar to the wok, and season to taste with salt and pepper. Simmer for a further 5 minutes, stirring occasionally.

Blend the cornflour with 1 tablespoon cold water to form a smooth paste and whisk into the soup. Return to the boil, then simmer over a medium heat until thickened.

Add the crab meat, stirring until blended. Beat the egg white with the chilli-flavoured oil and stir into the soup in a slow steady stream, stirring constantly. Stir in the chopped coriander and serve immediately.

Coconut Seafood

Serves 4

2 tbsp vegetable oil
450 g/1 lb raw king prawns,
peeled and deveined
2 bunches spring onions,
trimmed and thickly sliced
1 garlic clove, peeled and chopped
1 green chilli, deseeded and
finely chopped
2.5 cm/1 inch piece fresh
root ginger, peeled and cut
into matchsticks
125 g/4 oz fresh shiitake mushrooms,
rinsed and halved
150 ml/5 fl oz dry white wine
200 ml/7 fl oz carton coconut milk
4 tbsp freshly chopped coriander
salt and freshly ground black pepper
freshly cooked rice, to serve

Heat a large wok, add the oil and heat until it is almost smoking, swirling the oil around the wok to coat the sides. Add the prawns and stir-fry over a high heat for 4–5 minutes, or until browned on all sides. Using a slotted spoon, transfer the prawns to a plate and keep warm in a low oven.

Add the spring onion, garlic, chilli and ginger to the wok and stir-fry for 1 minute. Add the mushrooms and stir-fry for a further 3 minutes. Using a slotted spoon, transfer the mushroom mixture to a plate and keep warm in a low oven.

Add the wine and coconut milk to the wok, bring to the boil and boil rapidly for 4 minutes, until reduced slightly.

Return the mushroom mixture and prawns to the wok, bring back to the boil, then simmer for 1 minute, stirring occasionally, until piping hot. Stir in the freshly chopped coriander and season to taste with salt and pepper. Serve immediately with the freshly cooked rice.

Creamy Coconut Seafood Pasta

Serves 4

400 g/14 oz egg tagliatelle
1 tsp vegetable oil
1 tsp chilli-flavoured oil
4 spring onions, trimmed and
sliced diagonally
1 garlic clove, peeled and crushed
1 habañero chilli, deseeded
and finely chopped
2.5 cm/1 inch piece fresh root
ginger, peeled and grated
150 ml/5 fl oz coconut milk
100 ml/3^1/$_2$ fl oz double cream
225 g/8 oz cooked peeled
tiger prawns
185 g/6^1/$_2$ oz fresh white crab meat
2 tbsp freshly chopped coriander,
plus extra sprigs to garnish
salt and freshly ground
black pepper

Bring a large pan of lightly salted water to a rolling boil. Add the pasta and cook according to the packet instructions, or until *al dente*.

Meanwhile, heat the vegetable and chilli-flavoured oils together in a saucepan. Add the spring onion, garlic, chilli and ginger, and cook for 3–4 minutes, or until softened.

Blend the coconut milk and cream together in a jug. Add the prawns and crab meat to the pan and stir over a low heat for a few seconds to heat through. Gradually pour in the coconut cream mixture, stirring all the time.

Stir the chopped coriander into the seafood sauce and season to taste with salt and pepper. Continue heating the sauce gently until piping hot, but do not allow to boil.

Drain the pasta thoroughly and return to the pan. Add the seafood sauce and gently toss together to coat the pasta. Tip into a warmed serving dish or spoon onto individual plates. Serve immediately, garnished with coriander sprigs.

Grilled Snapper with Roasted Pepper

Serves 4

1 medium red pepper
1 medium green pepper
4–8 snapper fillets, depending on size, about 450 g/1 lb
1 tbsp olive oil
5 tbsp double cream
125 ml/4 fl oz white wine
1 tbsp freshly chopped dill, plus extra sprigs, to garnish
sea salt and freshly ground black pepper
freshly cooked tagliatelle, to serve

Preheat the grill to a high heat and line the bottom of the grill rack with foil. Cut the tops off the peppers and divide into quarters. Remove the seeds and membrane, then place on the foil-lined grill rack and cook for 8–10 minutes, turning frequently, until the skins have become charred and blackened. Remove from the grill rack, place in a polythene bag and leave until cool. When the peppers are cool, strip off and discard the skin. Slice the flesh thinly and reserve.

Cover the grill rack with another piece of foil, then place the snapper fillets skin-side up on the grill rack. Season to taste with salt and pepper, and brush with a little of the olive oil. Cook for 10–12 minutes, turning over once and brushing again with a little olive oil.

Pour the cream and wine into a small saucepan, bring to the boil and simmer for about 5 minutes until the sauce has thickened slightly. Add the chopped dill, season to taste and stir in the reserved peppers. Arrange the cooked snapper fillets on warm serving plates and pour over the cream and pepper sauce. Garnish with the extra dill sprigs and serve immediately with the freshly cooked tagliatelle.

Ackee Saltfish

Serves 4

450 g/1 lb salted cod
540 g/1lb 6 oz can ackee or
4 ripe ackee
25 g/1 oz butter
25 ml/1 fl oz vegetable oil
1 medium onion,
peeled and chopped
2–3 garlic cloves,
peeled and chopped
2 sprigs fresh thyme
225 g/8 oz ripe tomatoes
1 habañero chilli,
deseeded and sliced
1 tsp ground allspice
freshly ground black pepper
2 spring onions,
trimmed and chopped
fried dumplings or boiled green
bananas, to serve

Place the salted cod in a large bowl and cover with cold water. Leave for at least 24 hours, changing the water at least 6 times. Rinse thoroughly. When ready to cook, place in a saucepan and cover with cold water. Bring to the boil, then simmer for 15 minutes, or until tender.

If using canned ackee, drain when required. If using fresh, discard the seeds and pink membrane, wash the ackee thoroughly and place in medium saucepan. Cover with water and bring to the boil. Reduce the heat to a simmer and cook for 15–20 minutes, or until tender. Drain and reserve.

Remove the fish from the pan and immerse in cold water, then drain and leave until cool enough to handle. Once cool, remove and discard any bones and skin from the fish. Flake the flesh into small pieces and reserve.

Heat the butter and oil in a large frying pan over a medium heat. Add the onion and garlic. Once softened a little, add the thyme, tomato, chilli and allspice. Cook for 3–4 minutes, stirring frequently.

Add the flaked fish and cook for a further 5 minutes before adding the ackee. Cook for another 5–8 minutes, stirring carefully so as not to crush the ackee. Season to taste with the black pepper and sprinkle with the spring onion. Serve if liked with fried dumplings or boiled green bananas.

Creole Prawns Fettuccine

Serves 4

4 tbsp vegetable oil
450 g/1 lb raw tiger prawns, rinsed and peeled, shells and heads reserved
2 shallots, peeled and finely chopped
4 garlic cloves, peeled and finely chopped
1 habañero chilli, deseeded and finely chopped
large handful fresh basil leaves
1 carrot, peeled and finely chopped
1 onion, peeled and finely chopped
1 celery stick, trimmed and finely chopped
2 or 3 sprigs fresh parsley
2 or 3 sprigs fresh thyme
salt and freshly ground black pepper
pinch cayenne pepper
175 ml/6 fl oz dry white wine
450 g/1 lb ripe tomatoes, roughly chopped
juice of $^1/_2$ lemon, or to taste
350 g/12 oz fettuccine

Heat 2 tablespoons of the oil in a large saucepan over a high heat and add the prawn shells and heads. Fry for 2–3 minutes, until the shells turn pink and are lightly browned. Add half the shallot, half the garlic, the chilli, half the basil and the carrot, onion, celery, parsley and thyme. Season lightly with salt, pepper and cayenne, and sauté for 2–3 minutes, stirring often. Pour in the wine and stir, scraping the pan well. Bring to the boil, simmer for 1 minute, then add the tomato. Cook for a further 3–4 minutes. Pour in 200 ml/7 fl oz water. Bring to the boil, reduce the heat and simmer for about 30 minutes, stirring often. Use a wooden spoon to mash the shells and release their flavour. Lower the heat if the sauce is reducing too quickly. Strain through a sieve, pressing well to extract the liquid; there should be about 450 ml/15 fl oz. Pour into a clean pan and bring to the boil. Reduce the heat and simmer until reduced by about half.

Heat the remaining oil over a high heat in a clean frying pan and add the peeled prawns. Season lightly and add the lemon juice. Cook for 1 minute, lower the heat and add the remaining shallot and garlic. Cook for 1 minute. Add the sauce and adjust the seasoning.

Meanwhile, bring a large pan of lightly salted water to a rolling boil and add the fettuccine. Cook, or until al dente. Drain thoroughly. Transfer to a warmed serving dish, add the sauce and toss well. Garnish with the remaining basil and serve immediately.

Meat  Poultry

Many of the meat and poultry dishes of the Caribbean have been passed down through the generations, and hark back to the days before refrigeration. To prevent meat going bad in the hot tropical sun, a number of techniques were used, such as salting. Stewing meat to a point of melting succulence, marinating it in acidic liquids (such as vinegar or lemon juice) or rubbing it with hot spices are all ways of adding intense flavours or tenderizing tough meat.

Jamaican Jerk Pork with Rice & Peas

Serves 4

175 g/6 oz dried red kidney beans
2 onions, peeled and chopped
2 garlic cloves, peeled and crushed
4 tbsp lime juice
2 tbsp each dark molasses, soy sauce
and chopped fresh root ginger
2 jalapeño chillies,
deseeded and chopped
$^{1}/_{2}$ tsp ground cinnamon
$^{1}/_{4}$ tsp each ground allspice and
ground nutmeg
4 pork loin chops, on the bone
sprigs fresh flat-leaf parsley,
to garnish

For the rice:

1 tbsp vegetable oil
1 onion, peeled and finely chopped
1 celery stalk, trimmed and finely sliced
3 garlic cloves, peeled and crushed
2 bay leaves, fresh if possible
225 g/8 oz long-grain white rice
475 ml/16 fl oz chicken or ham stock

Soak the red kidney beans in plenty of cold water overnight.

To make the jerk pork marinade, purée the onion, garlic, lime juice, molasses, soy sauce, ginger, chilli, cinnamon, allspice and nutmeg together in a food processor until smooth. Put the pork chops into a plastic or non-reactive dish and pour over the marinade, turning the chops to coat. Marinate in the refrigerator for at least 1 hour or overnight.

Drain the beans and place in a large saucepan with about 2 litres/3$^{1}/_{2}$ pints cold water. Bring to the boil and continue boiling rapidly for 10 minutes. Reduce the heat, cover and simmer gently, for 1 hour until tender, adding more water if necessary. When cooked, drain well and mash roughly.

Heat the oil for the rice over a medium heat in a saucepan with a tight-fitting lid and add the onion, celery and garlic. Cook gently for 5 minutes until softened. Add the bay leaves, rice and stock, and stir. Bring to the boil, cover and cook very gently for 10 minutes. Add the beans and stir well again. Cook for a further 5 minutes, then remove from the heat.

Heat a griddle pan until almost smoking. Remove the pork chops from the marinade, scraping off any surplus, and add to the hot pan. Cook for 5–8 minutes on each side, or until cooked. Garnish with the parsley and serve immediately with the rice.

Pork Creole

Serves 4–6

For the jerk sauce:

2 tsp ground allspice; 50 g/2 oz light muscovado sugar; 6 garlic cloves, peeled; 2–4 Scotch bonnet chillies, deseeded; 2 tbsp freshly chopped thyme; 8 spring onions, trimmed and chopped; 1 tsp ground cinnamon; 1/4 tsp freshly grated nutmeg; salt and freshly ground black pepper; 2 tbsp soy sauce; 1 whole pork fillet, about 700 g/1 1/2 lb in weight

For the spicy rice:

1 tbsp olive oil; 2–3 garlic cloves, peeled and sliced; 1–2 red chillies, deseeded and chopped; 1–2 tbsp curry paste; 2 leeks, about 200 g/ 7 oz in weight, trimmed, sliced and washed; 300 g/10 oz basmati rice; 750 ml/1 1/4 pints vegetable stock; 225 g/8 oz French beans, trimmed and chopped; 1 large carrot, peeled and grated; 4 spring onions, trimmed and chopped; 2 tbsp fresh coriander

Preheat the oven to 190°C/375°F/Gas Mark 5. Place all the ingredients for the sauce in a food processor and blend until smooth.

Trim the fillet and, if liked, cut in half. Place the meat in a shallow roasting tin and brush with the prepared sauce. Cover lightly and store in the refrigerator until required. When ready to cook, remove the meat from the refrigerator, allow to return to room temperature, then place in the preheated oven and roast for 30 minutes, or until thoroughly cooked. Slice and keep warm.

Meanwhile, heat the oil in a large frying pan, add the garlic, chillies, curry paste and leeks and cook, stirring, for 5 minutes before adding the rice. Continue to cook, stirring, for a further 5 minutes.

Add half the stock, bring to the boil, then reduce the heat, cover and simmer for 10 minutes, stirring frequently. Add the chopped beans together with a little more stock and cook for a further 10 minutes, or until the rice is tender. Add more stock as necessary. Stir in the carrot, black pepper to taste and spring onions. Sprinkle with chopped coriander and serve with the sliced pork fillet.

Caribbean Pork

Serves 4

450 g/1 lb pork fillet
2.5 cm/1 inch piece fresh root
ginger, peeled and grated
1/2 tsp crushed dried chillies
2 garlic cloves, peeled and crushed
2 tbsp freshly chopped parsley
150 ml/5 fl oz pint orange juice
2 tbsp dark soy sauce
2 tbsp vegetable oil
1 large onion, peeled and
sliced into wedges
1 large courgette (about 225 g/8 oz),
trimmed and cut into strips
1 orange pepper, deseeded and
cut into strips
1 ripe but firm mango
freshly cooked rice, to serve

Cut the pork fillet into thin strips and place in a shallow dish. Sprinkle with the ginger, chilli, garlic and half the parsley. Blend together the orange juice, soy sauce and 1 tablespoon of the oil, then pour over the pork. Cover and chill in the refrigerator for 30 minutes, stirring occasionally. Remove the pork strips with a slotted spoon and reserve the marinade.

Heat the wok over a medium heat until hot, then add the remaining oil and heat until just beginning to smoke. Stir-fry the pork for 3–4 minutes. Add the onion courgette and pepper strips, and cook for 2 minutes. Add the reserved marinade to the wok and stir-fry for a further 2 minutes.

Peel the mango and remove the stone. Cut the flesh into strips, then stir it into the pork mixture. Continue to stir-fry until everything is piping hot. Garnish with the remaining parsley and serve immediately with plenty of freshly cooked rice.

Sticky Braised Spare Ribs

Serves 4

900 g/2 lb meaty pork spare ribs, cut
crossways into 7.5 cm/3 inch pieces
125 ml/4 fl oz mango juice or
orange juice
50 ml/2 fl oz dry white wine
1–2 tbsp hot pepper sauce
3 tbsp tomato ketchup
2 tbsp clear honey
1 tbsp black treacle
3 or 4 spring onions, trimmed
and chopped, plus extra, cut into
tassels, to garnish
2 garlic cloves, peeled and crushed
grated zest of 1 small orange
salt and freshly ground black pepper
lemon wedges, to garnish

Put the spare ribs in the wok and add enough cold water to cover. Bring to the boil over a medium-high heat, skimming off any scum that rises to the surface. Cover and simmer for 30 minutes, then drain and rinse the ribs.

Rinse and dry the wok, then return the ribs to it. In a bowl, blend the fruit juice with the white wine, hot pepper sauce, tomato ketchup, honey and treacle until smooth. Stir in the spring onions, garlic and orange zest. Stir well until mixed thoroughly. Pour the mixture over the spare ribs and stir gently until the ribs are lightly coated. Place the wok over a moderate heat and bring the ribs to the boil.

Cover then simmer, stirring occasionally, for 1 hour, or until the ribs are tender and the sauce is thickened and sticky. (If the sauce reduces too quickly or begins to stick, add a little water a tablespoon at a time until the ribs are tender.) Adjust the seasoning to taste, then transfer the ribs to a serving plate and garnish with spring onion tassels and lemon wedges. Serve immediately.

Pepper-pot Stew

Serves 4–6

450 g/1 lb lean pork, such as fillet
225 g/8 oz lean braising steak
2 tbsp vegetable oil
1 onion, peeled and chopped
2 celery stalks, trimmed and sliced
4 garlic cloves, peeled and chopped
1–2 habanero chillies,
deseeded and chopped
1 tsp allspice
$\frac{1}{2}$ tsp ground cloves
1 tsp ground cinnamon
450 g/1 lb ripe tomatoes, chopped
1 tbsp tomato purée
300 ml/$\frac{1}{2}$ pint beef stock
salt and freshly ground black pepper
hot pepper sauce, to taste (optional)
1 tbsp freshly chopped coriander

To serve:

sweet chutney
freshly cooked rice
freshly cooked peas

Trim the pork and beef discarding any fat or gristle, cut into thin strips and reserve. Heat the oil in a large saucepan, add the onion, celery and garlic and sauté for 5 minutes, or until beginning to soften. Add the chillies and spices and continue to cook for 3 minutes before adding the meat strips.

Cook, stirring, until the meat is coated in the spices, then stir in the chopped tomatoes. Blend the tomato purée with a little stock and stir into the pan with the remaining stock. Bring to the boil, then reduce the heat, cover and simmer, stirring occasionally, for 1$\frac{1}{2}$–2 hours, or until the meat is tender. If the liquid is evaporating too quickly, reduce the heat and add a little more stock.

Adjust the seasoning, adding some hot pepper sauce, if liked, and sprinkle with chopped coriander. Serve with a sweet chutney and freshly cooked rice and peas.

Speedy Pork with Yellow Bean Sauce

Serves 4

450 g/1 lb pork fillet
2 tbsp light soy sauce
1 tsp chilli powder
2 tbsp mango juice
2 tsp cornflour
3 tbsp vegetable oil
2 garlic cloves, peeled and crushed
175 g/6 oz carrots, peeled and cut into matchsticks
125 g/4 oz fine green beans, trimmed and halved
2 spring onions, trimmed and cut into strips
4 tbsp yellow bean sauce
1 tbsp freshly chopped flat-leaf parsley, to garnish
freshly cooked egg noodles, to serve

Remove any fat or sinew from the pork fillet, and cut into thin strips. Blend the soy sauce, chilli powder, mango juice and cornflour in a bowl and mix thoroughly. Place the meat in a glass or ceramic bowl, pour over the soy sauce mixture, cover and leave to marinate in the refrigerator for 1 hour. Drain with a slotted spoon, reserving the marinade.

Heat a wok over a medium heat until hot, then add 2 tablespoons of the oil and heat until just beginning to smoke. Stir-fry the pork with the garlic for 2 minutes, or until the meat is sealed. Remove with a slotted spoon and reserve.

Add the remaining oil to the wok and cook the carrot, beans and spring onion for about 3 minutes, until tender but still crisp. Return the pork to the wok with the reserved marinade, then pour over the yellow bean sauce. Stir-fry for a further 1–2 minutes, or until the pork is tender. Sprinkle with the chopped parsley and serve immediately with freshly cooked egg noodles.

Jerked Steaks

Serves 4–6

4 rump/sirloin steaks, *c.* 100 g/4 oz each

For the jerk sauce:
1 tsp ground allspice; 25 g/1 oz light muscovado sugar; 1–2 garlic cloves, peeled and chopped; 1 small red chilli, deseeded and chopped; few fresh thyme sprigs, leaves removed; 1 tsp ground cinnamon; $1/4$ tsp freshly grated nutmeg; salt and freshly ground black pepper; 1 tbsp soy sauce

For the mango relish:
1 ripe mango, peeled, stoned and finely chopped; 6 spring onions, trimmed and chopped; 1–2 garlic cloves, peeled and crushed; 1 red chilli, deseeded and chopped; 1 small, ripe but firm banana, peeled and chopped; 1 tbsp lime juice; 1 tbsp clear honey, warmed; 50 g/2 oz unsweetened chopped dates; 1 tsp ground cinnamon

Blend all the ingredients for the jerk sauce then rub over the steaks. Place on a plate, lightly cover and leave in the refrigerator for at least 30 minutes.

Mix together all the ingredients for the mango relish, cover and leave for 30 minutes to allow the flavours to develop.

When ready to cook, heat a griddle pan or heavy-based frying pan until hot and a few drops of water sizzle when dropped into the pan. Add the steaks and cook for 2–3 minutes on each side for rare, 3–4 minutes on each side for medium and 5–6 minutes on each side for well done.

Remove from the pan and serve with the prepared relish, salad and potato wedges.

Coconut Beef

Serves 4

450 g/1 lb beef rump or sirloin steak,
trimmed and cut into thin strips
2 tbsp groundnut oil
2 bunches spring onions,
trimmed and thickly sliced
1 habañero chilli,
deseeded and chopped
1 garlic clove, peeled and chopped
2 cm/1 inch piece fresh root ginger,
peeled and cut into matchsticks
125 g/4 oz shiitake mushrooms
(or closed cup if preferred, for a
less Oriental feel)
200 ml/7 fl oz coconut cream
150 ml/¼ pint beef stock
4 tbsp freshly chopped coriander
salt and freshly ground black pepper
freshly cooked rice, to serve

Heat a wok or large frying pan, add 1 tablespoon of the oil and heat until just smoking. Add the beef and cook for 5–8 minutes, turning occasionally, until browned on all sides. Using a slotted spoon, transfer the beef to a plate and keep warm.

Add the remaining oil to the wok and heat until almost smoking. Add the spring onion, chilli, garlic and ginger and cook for 1 minute, stirring occasionally. Add the mushroom and stir-fry for 3 minutes. Using a slotted spoon, transfer the mushroom mixture to a plate and keep warm.

Return the beef to the wok, pour in the coconut cream and stock. Bring to the boil and simmer for 3–4 minutes, or until the juices are slightly reduced and the beef is just tender.

Return the mushroom mixture to the wok and heat through. Stir in the coriander and season to taste with salt and pepper. Serve immediately with freshly cooked rice.

Jamaican Jerk Chicken

Serves 4

For the jerk seasoning:

1 tsp ground allspice
1 tsp ground cinnamon
1/2 tsp freshly grated nutmeg
1 tsp dried thyme
1 tsp garlic powder
1 hot chilli, such as Scotch bonnet,
deseeded and finely chopped
2 tbsp vegetable oil
1 tbsp butter, melted
2 tbsp chicken stock
1 tbsp tomato purée
2 tbsp lime juice
1 tbsp white wine vinegar
1–2 tsp muscovado sugar
1/2 tsp freshly ground black pepper
4–8 chicken portions, depending
on size
grilled pineapple and lime wedges,
to serve (optional)

Put all the jerk seasoning ingredients into a glass mixing bowl and mash together until thoroughly blended.

Rinse the chicken and pat dry with absorbent kitchen paper. Make a few cuts across the skin of the chicken, then place in a shallow dish. Spoon the jerk seasoning over the chicken and leave to marinate in the refrigerator for at least 4 hours; longer if time permits. Brush the chicken with the marinade or turn over occasionally during this time.

When ready to cook preheat the oven to 190˚C/375˚F/ Gas Mark 5. Place the chicken on a baking tray, and brush with the marinade left in the dish. Cook in the oven for 25–30 minutes, or until the chicken is thoroughly cooked and the juices run clear when the flesh is pierced with a sharp knife. Serve with grilled pineapple and lime wedges, if liked.

Spicy Chicken Skewers with Mango Tipili

Serves 4

400 g/14 oz chicken breast fillet
200 ml/7 fl oz plain yogurt
1 garlic clove, peeled and crushed
1 hot red chilli, deseeded and finely chopped
$1/2$ tsp ground turmeric
finely grated zest and juice of $1/2$ lemon
fresh mint sprigs, to garnish

For the tipili:

175 g/6 oz bulgur wheat
1 tsp olive oil
juice of $1/2$ lemon
$1/2$ red onion, finely chopped
1 ripe mango, halved, stoned, peeled and chopped
$1/4$ cucumber, finely diced
2 tbsp freshly chopped parsley
2 tbsp freshly shredded mint
salt and finely ground black pepper

If using wooden skewers, soak them in cold water for at least 30 minutes before using. (This stops them from burning during grilling.)

Cut the chicken into 5 x 1 cm/2 x $1/2$ inch strips and place in a shallow dish. Mix together the yogurt, garlic, chilli, turmeric, lemon zest and juice. Pour over the chicken and toss to coat. Cover and leave to marinate in the refrigerator for up to 8 hours.

To make the tipili, put the bulgur wheat in a bowl. Pour over enough boiling water to cover. Put a plate over the bowl. Leave to soak for 20 minutes. Whisk together the oil and lemon juice in a bowl. Add the red onion and leave to marinate for 10 minutes.

Drain the bulgur wheat and squeeze out any excess moisture in a clean tea towel. Add to the red onion with the mango, cucumber, parsley and mint. Season to taste with salt and pepper. Toss together.

Thread the chicken strips onto eight wooden or metal skewers. Cook under a hot grill for 8 minutes. Turn and brush with the marinade, until the chicken is lightly browned and cooked through.

Spoon the bulgur salad onto individual plates. Arrange the chicken skewers on top and garnish with the mint sprigs. Serve warm or cold.

Hot Spicy Chicken

Serves 4

4 chicken portions
3 tbsp plain flour
$^1/_2$ tsp hot paprika
2 tsp sunflower oil
1 small onion, peeled and chopped
1 Scotch bonnet red chilli,
deseeded and finely chopped
$^1/_2$ tsp ground cumin
$^1/_2$ tsp dried oregano
300 ml/10 fl oz chicken or
vegetable stock
1 green pepper,
deseeded and sliced
2 tsp cocoa powder
1 tbsp lime juice
2 tsp clear honey
3 tbsp Greek-style yogurt
salt and freshly ground black pepper
lime slices, to garnish
red chilli slices, to garnish
sprig of fresh oregano, to garnish
freshly cooked rice, to serve
green salad leaves, to serve

Using a knife, remove the skin from the chicken joints. In a shallow dish, mix together the flour, paprika, salt and pepper. Coat the chicken on both sides with the flour and shake off any excess if necessary. Heat the oil over a medium heat in a large nonstick frying pan. Add the chicken and brown on both sides. Transfer to a plate and reserve.

Add the onion and red chilli to the pan, and gently cook for 5 minutes, or until the onion is soft. Stir occasionally. Stir in the cumin and oregano, and cook for a further minute. Pour in the stock and bring to the boil.

Return the chicken to the pan, cover and cook for 40 minutes. Add the green pepper and cook for a further 10 minutes, or until the chicken is cooked. Remove the chicken and pepper with a slotted spoon and keep warm in a serving dish.

Blend the cocoa powder with 1 tablespoon warm water. Stir into the sauce, then boil rapidly until the sauce has thickened and reduced by about one third. Stir in the lime juice, honey and yogurt.

Pour the sauce over the chicken and pepper, and garnish with the lime slices, chilli and oregano. Serve immediately with the freshly cooked rice and salad leaves.

Caribbean-style Chicken Stew

Serves 4–6

4 skinless, boneless chicken portions,
each about 100 g/4 oz in weight
2 tbsp groundnut oil
2 celery stalks, trimmed
6 baby onions, peeled and halved
2–4 garlic cloves, peeled and sliced
1–2 Habanero chillies,
deseeded and sliced
1 tsp ground cumin
1 tsp ground coriander
1 tsp ground allspice
1 tsp turmeric
2 tsp demerara sugar
225 g/8 oz tomatoes, chopped
600 ml/1 pint chicken stock
1 tbsp freshly chopped coriander
sweet potato mash, to serve

Lightly rinse the chicken and dry with absorbent kitchen paper. Heat the oil in a large saucepan, add the chicken and brown on all sides. Remove and reserve.

Chop the celery and add to the pan with the onions, garlic and chillies. Sauté for 5–8 minutes, or until lightly browned. Add all the spices and cook for a further 3 minutes. Add the sugar, tomatoes and stock and bring to the boil.

Return the chicken to the pan, then reduce the heat, cover and simmer for 1 hour, or until the chicken is tender. Spoon into a warmed serving dish, sprinkle with chopped coriander and serve with the sweet potato mash.

Chicken Pie with Sweet Potato Topping

Serves 4

700 g/1¹/₂ lb sweet potatoes,
peeled and cut into chunks
250 g/9 oz potatoes, peeled and
cut into chunks
150 ml/5 fl oz milk
25 g/1 oz butter
2 tsp soft brown sugar
grated zest of 1 orange
4 skinless chicken breast fillets, diced
1 medium onion, peeled and
coarsely chopped
125 g/4 oz baby mushrooms,
stems trimmed
2 leeks, trimmed and thickly sliced
150 ml/5 fl oz dry white wine
1 chicken stock cube
1 tbsp freshly chopped parsley
50 ml/2 fl oz crème fraîche or
thick double cream
salt and freshly ground
black pepper
fresh green vegetables, to serve

Cook both lots of potatoes in lightly salted boiling water until tender. Drain well, then return to the saucepan and mash until smooth and creamy, gradually adding the milk, then the butter, sugar and orange zest. Season to taste with salt and pepper, and reserve.

Put the chicken in a saucepan with the onion, mushrooms, leeks, wine and stock cube. Season to taste. Simmer, covered, for 15–20 minutes or until the chicken and vegetables are tender. Using a slotted spoon, transfer the chicken and vegetables to a 1.1 litre/2 pint pie dish. Add the parsley and crème fraîche to the liquid in the pan and bring to the boil. Simmer until thickened and smooth, stirring constantly. Pour over the chicken in the pie dish, mix and cool.

Preheat the oven to 190°C/375°F/Gas Mark 5. Spread the mashed potato over the chicken filling, and swirl the surface into decorative peaks. Bake in the oven for 35 minutes, or until the top is golden and the chicken filling is heated through. Serve immediately with the green vegetables.

Calypso Chicken

Serves 4–6

2 onions
2 tbsp groundnut oil
450 g/1 lb skinless, boneless
chicken breast, diced
2–4 garlic cloves, peeled and sliced
1–2 chillies, deseeded and sliced
1 tsp ground coriander
1 tsp ground cumin
1 tsp turmeric
1 tsp ground allspice
400 ml/14 fl oz coconut milk
200 ml/7 fl oz chicken stock
1 large red pepper,
deseeded and diced
1 green pepper,
deseeded and diced
15 g/$\frac{1}{2}$ oz coconut chips, toasted
or 1 tbsp freshly chopped
coriander, to garnish
freshly cooked rice, to serve

Peel the onions and, keeping the root intact, cut into thin wedges. Heat the oil in a heavy-based saucepan, add the chicken and brown on all sides. Remove from the pan and reserve.

Add the onions, garlic and chillies to the pan and sauté for 5–8 minutes, or until lightly browned. Sprinkle in all the spices and cook, stirring, for 2 minutes.

Return the chicken to the pan and stir in the coconut milk and stock. Bring to the boil, then reduce the heat, cover and simmer for 30 minutes.

Add the peppers and continue to simmer for 15 minutes, or until the chicken is cooked. Spoon into a warmed serving dish, sprinkle with toasted coconut or chopped coriander and serve with rice.

Creamy Caribbean Chicken Coconut Soup

Serves 4

175 g/6 oz cooked chicken, shredded or diced
6–8 spring onions, trimmed and thinly sliced
2 garlic cloves, peeled and finely chopped
1 red chilli, deseeded and finely chopped
2 tbsp vegetable oil
1 tsp ground turmeric
300 ml/$^1/_2$ pint coconut milk
900 ml/1 $^1/_2$ pints chicken stock
50 g/2 oz small soup pasta or spaghetti, broken into small pieces
$^1/_2$ lemon, sliced
1–2 tbsp freshly chopped coriander, plus extra sprigs, to garnish
salt and freshly ground black pepper

Heat a large wok, add the oil and, when hot, add the spring onion, garlic and chilli. Stir-fry for 2 minutes, or until the onion has softened. Stir in the turmeric and cook for 1 minute.

Blend the coconut milk with the chicken stock until smooth, then pour into the wok. Add the pasta with the lemon slices and bring to the boil. Simmer, half-covered, for 10–12 minutes, or until the pasta is tender; stir occasionally.

Remove the lemon slices from the wok and add the chicken. Season to taste with salt and pepper, and simmer for 2–3 minutes, or until the chicken is heated through thoroughly. Stir in the chopped coriander and ladle into heated bowls. Garnish with the extra sprigs of coriander and serve immediately.

Chicken in Black Bean Sauce

Serves 4

450 g/1 lb skinless, boneless chicken
breast fillets, cut into strips
1 tbsp light soy sauce
2 tbsp dry sherry or rum
a little salt
1 tsp caster sugar
1 tsp chilli-flavoured oil
2–3 tsp hot pepper sauce, plus extra,
to taste
2 tsp cornflour
2 tbsp sunflower oil
2 green peppers,
deseeded and diced
1 tbsp freshly grated root ginger
2 garlic cloves, peeled and
roughly chopped
2 shallots, peeled and finely chopped
4 spring onions, trimmed and finely
sliced, plus extra, shredded,
to garnish
3 tbsp salted black beans, chopped
150 ml/5 fl oz pint chicken stock
freshly cooked egg noodles,
to serve

Place the chicken strips in a large bowl. Mix together the soy sauce, salt, caster sugar, chilli oil, 2–3 teaspoons hot pepper sauce and the cornflour. Pour over the chicken.

Heat the wok over a high heat, add the sunflower oil and, when very hot, add the chicken strips and stir-fry for 2 minutes. Add the green pepper and stir-fry for a further 2 minutes. Next add the ginger, garlic, shallot, sliced spring onion and black beans, and continue to stir-fry for another 2 minutes.

Add 4 tablespoons of the stock and stir-fry for 1 minute, then pour in the remaining stock and bring to the boil. Reduce the heat and simmer the sauce for 3–4 minutes, until the chicken is cooked and the sauce has thickened slightly. Garnish with the shredded spring onion and serve immediately with the egg noodles.

Tropical Sautéed Chicken Curry

Serves 4–6

2 tbsp groundnut oil
4 garlic cloves, peeled and chopped
2 red onions, peeled and cut
into wedges
5 cm/2 inch piece fresh root ginger,
peeled and grated
2 green chillies, deseeded and sliced
1 tbsp finely grated lime zest
450 g/1 lb skinless, boneless
chicken, diced
2 tsp demerara sugar
1 tbsp Madras curry paste
4 tbsp rum
150 ml/^{1}/$_4$ pint chicken stock
150 ml/^{1}/$_4$ pint coconut milk
350 g/12 oz butternut squash, peeled,
deseeded and cut into chunks
1 large or 2 small firm but ripe
papaya, peeled, deseeded
and sliced
3 tbsp lime juice
2 small firm bananas, peeled and
cut into strips
2 tbsp freshly chopped coriander

Heat the oil in a large frying pan, add the garlic, onions, ginger, chillies and lime zest and fry for 5 minutes, or until beginning to soften.

Add the chicken and cook, stirring, until sealed and coated lightly in the garlic and chilli mixture. Add the sugar and curry paste and cook, stirring, for 3 minutes.

Pour in the rum and heat for 1 minute. Take off the heat and ignite. When the flames have subsided pour in the stock and coconut milk. Return to the heat, bring to the boil, stirring occasionally, then add the butternut squash.

Reduce the heat, cover and simmer for 25 minutes, stirring occasionally. Add the papaya, lime juice and bananas and continue to simmer for 10–15 minutes, or until the chicken and squash are thoroughly cooked. Sprinkle with chopped coriander and serve.

Duck Exotic Fruit Stir-fry

Serves 4

4 duck breast fillets, skin removed
and cut into strips
1 tbsp hot pepper sauce
2 tbsp light soy sauce
1 tbsp chilli-flavoured oil
1 tbsp groundnut oil
2 celery stalks, trimmed and diced
1 small fresh pineapple, peeled and
cut into chunks, or 225 g/
8 oz can pineapple chunks, drained
1 mango, peeled, stoned
and cut into chunks
125 g/4 oz lychees, peeled if fresh,
stoned and halved
125 ml/4 fl oz chicken stock
2 tbsp tomato purée
2 tbsp mango chutney
2 tsp wine vinegar
pinch soft brown sugar
steamed rice, to serve

Place the duck strips in a shallow bowl. Mix together the hot pepper sauce, soy sauce and chilli-flavoured oil. Pour over the duck and marinate for 2 hours in the refrigerator. Stir occasionally during marinating. Remove the duck from the marinade.

Heat the wok, add the groundnut oil and, when hot, stir-fry the marinated duck strips for 4 minutes. Remove from the wok and reserve.

Add the celery to the wok and stir-fry for 2 minutes, then add the pineapple, mango and lychees, and stir-fry for a further 3 minutes. Return the duck to the wok.

Mix together the chicken stock, tomato purée, mango chutney, wine vinegar and brown sugar. Add to the wok, bring to the boil and simmer, stirring, for 2 minutes. Serve immediately with the freshly steamed rice.

Spicy Chicken Pasta Salad

Serves 6

450 g/1 lb pasta shells
25 g/1 oz butter
1 onion, peeled and chopped
2 tbsp mild curry paste
125 g/4 oz ready-to-eat dried
apricots, chopped
2 tbsp tomato purée
3 tbsp mango chutney
300 ml/10 fl oz mayonnaise
1 ripe medium fresh pineapple
salt and freshly ground
black pepper
450 g/1 lb skinned and
boned cooked chicken,
cut into bite-size pieces
25 g/1 oz flaked toasted
almond slivers
coriander sprigs, to garnish

Bring a large pan of lightly salted water to a rolling boil. Add the pasta shells and cook according to the packet instructions, or until *al dente*. Drain and refresh under cold running water then drain thoroughly and place in a large serving bowl.

Meanwhile, melt the butter in a heavy-based pan, add the onion and cook for 5 minutes, or until softened. Add the curry paste and cook, stirring, for 2 minutes. Stir in the apricots and tomato purée, then cook for 1 minute. Remove from the heat and allow to cool.

Blend the mango chutney and mayonnaise together in a small bowl. Discard the plume from the pineapple. Stand on a chopping board and cut away and discard the skin. Cut the flesh into rings then cut out the central core using a sharp knife or metal cutter. Reserve any juice. Add the reserved pineapple juice to the mayonnaise mixture. Season the mayonnaise mixture to taste with salt and pepper.

Cut the pineapple slices into chunks and stir into the pasta together with the mayonnaise mixture, curry paste and cooked chicken pieces. Toss lightly together to coat the pasta. Sprinkle with the almond slivers, garnish with coriander sprigs and serve.

Desserts

There is an abundant supply of sweet, tangy and juicy tropical fruits in the Caribbean, so it is no surprise that fresh fruit features heavily in island dessert menus. Creating these heavenly treats at home is easier than ever before, thanks to the increased availability of unusual fruits, such as guavas, papayas and mangoes. Few desserts, however, evoke the spirit of Caribbean cuisine as indulgently as bananas fried in butter, sugar, rum and fruit juice. Enjoy!

Coconut Cake

Makes 10–12 slices

275 g/10 oz plain flour
2 tbsp cornflour
1 tbsp baking powder
1 tsp salt
150 g/5 oz white vegetable fat or
soft margarine
275 g/10 oz caster sugar
grated zest of 2 lemons
1 tsp vanilla extract
3 large eggs
150 ml/$\frac{1}{4}$ pint milk
4 tbsp Malibu or rum
450 g/1 lb jar lemon curd
lime zest, to decorate

For the frosting:

275 g/10 oz caster sugar
125 ml/4 fl oz water
1 tbsp glucose
$\frac{1}{4}$ tsp salt
1 tsp vanilla extract
3 large egg whites
75 g/3 oz shredded coconut

Preheat the oven to 180°C/350°F/Gas Mark 4, 10 minutes before baking. Lightly oil and flour two 20.5 cm/8 inch nonstick cake tins. Sift the flour, cornflour, baking powder and salt into a large bowl and add the vegetable fat or margarine, sugar, lemon zest, vanilla, eggs and milk. With an electric whisk on a low speed, beat until blended, adding a little extra milk if the mixture is very stiff. Increase the speed to medium and beat for about 2 minutes. Divide the mixture between the tins and smooth the tops evenly. Bake in the oven for 20–25 minutes until the cakes feel firm and are cooked. Remove from the oven and cool before turning out.

Put all the ingredients for the frosting, except the coconut, into a heatproof bowl placed over a saucepan of simmering water. (Do not allow the base of the bowl to touch the water.) Using an electric whisk, blend on a low speed. Increase the speed to high and beat for 7 minutes, until the whites are stiff and glossy. Remove the bowl from the heat and continue beating until cool. Cover with clingfilm.

Using a serrated knife, split the cake layers horizontally in half and sprinkle each cut surface with the Malibu or rum. Sandwich the cakes together with the lemon curd and press lightly. Spread the top and sides generously with the frosting, swirling and peaking the top. Sprinkle the coconut over the top of the cake and gently press on to the sides to cover. Decorate the coconut cake with the lime zest and serve.

Banana Cake

Cuts into 8 slices

3 ripe bananas
1 tsp lemon juice
150 g/5 oz soft brown sugar
75 g/3 oz butter or margarine
250 g/9 oz self-raising flour
2 tsp ground cinnamon
3 medium eggs
50 g/2 oz walnuts, chopped
1 tsp caster sugar
fresh cream, to serve

Preheat the oven to 190°C/375°F/Gas Mark 5. Lightly oil and line the bottom of an 18 cm/7 inch deep round cake tin with greaseproof or baking paper.

Mash 2 of the bananas in a small bowl, sprinkle with the lemon juice and a heaped tablespoon of the brown sugar. Mix together lightly and reserve.

Gently heat the remaining brown sugar and butter in a small saucepan until the butter has just melted. Pour into a bowl, and allow to cool slightly.

Sift the flour and teaspoon of the cinnamon into a large bowl and make a well in the centre.

Beat the eggs into the cooled sugar mixture, then pour into the well of flour and mix thoroughly. Gently stir in the mashed banana mixture. Pour half of the mixture into the prepared tin. Thinly slice the remaining banana and arrange over the cake mixture. Sprinkle over the walnuts, then cover with the remaining cake mixture.

Bake in the oven for 50–55 minutes, or until well risen and golden brown. Allow to cool in the tin, turn out and sprinkle with the remaining ground cinnamon and the caster sugar. Serve hot or cold with a jug of fresh cream for pouring.

Carrot Cake

Cuts into 8 slices

200 g/7 oz plain flour
$^1/_2$ tsp ground cinnamon
$^1/_2$ tsp freshly grated nutmeg
1 tsp baking powder
1 tsp bicarbonate of soda
175 g/6 oz unsalted butter, softened
150 g/5 oz dark muscovado sugar
3 medium eggs
2 ripe bananas, peeled and mashed
225 g/8 oz carrots, peeled and
roughly grated
50 g/2 oz chopped walnuts
1–2 tbsp rum

For the icing:

175 g/6 oz cream cheese
finely grated zest of 1 orange
1 tbsp orange juice
1 tsp vanilla extract
125 g/4 oz icing sugar

Preheat the oven to 150°C/300°F/Gas Mark 2. Lightly oil and line the bottom of a 15 cm/6 inch deep square cake tin with greaseproof or baking paper.

Sift the flour, baking powder and bicarbonate of soda together into a large bowl. Beat the muscovado sugar and butter together until soft and creamy. Add the eggs to the butter and sugar mixture, then gradually stir in the flour mixture. Combine well.

Add the banana, carrots, walnuts and rum. Mix lightly together to give a soft dripping consistency, then pour into the prepared cake tin. Bake in the oven for 1$^1/_4$ hours, or until light and springy to the touch and a skewer inserted into the centre of the cake comes out clean. Remove from the oven and allow to cool in the tin for 5 minutes before turning out on to a wire rack. Allow to cool completely, then remove and discard the lining paper.

To make the icing, beat together the cream cheese, orange zest, orange juice and vanilla extract. Sift the icing sugar and stir into the cream cheese mixture. Spread the cream cheese icing over the top of the cake and serve cut into squares.

White Chocolate & Passion Fruit Cake

Cuts into 8–10 slices

125 g/4 oz white chocolate, plus
125 g/4 oz extra, coarsely grated,
to decorate
125 g/4 oz butter
225 g/8 oz caster sugar
2 medium eggs
125 ml/4 fl oz sour cream
200 g/7 oz plain flour, sifted
75 g/3 oz self-raising flour, sifted

For the icing:

200 g/7 oz caster sugar
4 tbsp passion fruit juice (about 8–10
passion fruit, sieved)
1 1/2 tbsp passion fruit pulp
250 g/9 oz unsalted butter

Preheat the oven to 180°C/350°F/Gas Mark 4. Lightly oil and line two 20.5 cm/8 inch cake tins with greaseproof paper. Melt 125 g/4 oz white chocolate in a heatproof bowl set over a saucepan of simmering water. Stir in 125 ml/4 fl oz warm water and stir. Leave to cool.

Whisk the butter and sugar together until light and fluffy. Add the eggs, one at a time, beating well after each addition. Beat in the chocolate mixture, sour cream and sifted flours. Divide the mixture into eight. Spread one portion into each of the tins. Bake in the oven for 10 minutes, or until firm, then turn out onto wire racks. Repeat, to make eight cake layers.

To make the icing, put 125 ml/4 fl oz water and 50 g/2 oz of the sugar in a saucepan. Heat gently, stirring, until the sugar has dissolved. Bring to the boil and simmer for 2 minutes. Remove from the heat and cool, then add 2 tablespoons of the passion fruit juice. Reserve. Blend the remaining sugar with 50 ml/2 fl oz water in a small saucepan and stir constantly over a low heat, without boiling, until the sugar has dissolved. Remove from the heat and cool. Stir in the remaining passion fruit juice and the pulp. Cool, then strain. Using an electric whisk, beat the butter in a bowl until very pale. Gradually beat in the syrup. Place one layer of cake on a serving plate. Brush with the syrup and spread with a thin layer of icing. Repeat with the remaining cake, syrup and icing, ending with a final layer of icing on top. Press the grated chocolate into the top and sides.

Caribbean Rum Cake

Cuts into 12 slices

100 g/4 oz ready-to-eat dried
papaya, finely chopped
100 g/4 oz ready-to-eat dried
pineapple, finely chopped
100 g/4 oz ready-to-eat dried
mango, finely chopped
225 g/8 oz sultanas
225 g/8 oz raisins
8 tbsp rum
225 g/8 oz unsalted butter, softened
225 g/ 8 oz light muscovado sugar
1 tsp ground cinnamon
1 tsp ground allspice
1/2 tsp freshly grated nutmeg
4 medium eggs, beaten
300 g/10 oz self-raising flour

For the topping:
2–3 tbsp shredded coconut
2 tbsp ground almonds
350 g/12 oz ready-to-eat
dried fruits, cut into chunks
50 g/2 oz sugar; 4 tbsp rum

Preheat the oven to 180°C/350°F/Gas Mark 4. Lightly oil and line a 20.5 cm/8 inch deep cake tin with greaseproof or baking paper. Place the dried fruits for the cake in a bowl. Warm the rum, then pour over the fruits and leave to marinate for at least 1 hour; longer if time permits.

Cream the butter, sugar and spices until light and fluffy. Gradually add the eggs, beating well and adding a spoonful of flour after each addition. When all the eggs have been added, stir in the remaining flour. Add the soaked dried fruit and rum. Stir together to give a soft dropping consistency. Spoon into the prepared cake tin and level the top. Mix the coconut and ground almonds for the topping together and sprinkle over the top. Bake in the oven for 20 minutes, then arrange the fruits for the topping attractively on top. Continue to bake for a further 1 hour 20 minutes, or until a skewer inserted into the centre comes out clean. Cover the top with foil about 20 minutes after arranging the fruits on top.

Meanwhile, put the 50 g/2 oz sugar in a heavy-based saucepan with the 4 tablespoons rum. Heat gently until the sugar has dissolved, then bring to the boil and continue to boil steadily for 2–3 minutes until a light syrup is formed. Reserve. Once the cake is cooked, warm the syrup slightly, then slowly pour over the cake. Allow to cool in the tin before turning out and discarding the lining paper. This cake is best if left for 2–3 days before cutting. Store in an airtight tin.

Fruity Chocolate Bread Pudding

Serves 4

175 g/6 oz plain dark chocolate
1 small fruit loaf
125 g/4 oz ready-to-eat dried
apricots, roughly chopped
450 ml³/₄ pint single cream
300 ml/¹/₂ pint milk
1 tbsp caster sugar
3 medium eggs
3 tbsp demerara sugar, for
sprinkling

Preheat the oven to 180°C/ 350°F/Gas Mark 4, 10 minutes before cooking. Lightly butter a shallow ovenproof dish. Break the chocolate into small pieces and place in a heatproof bowl set over a saucepan of gently simmering water. Heat gently, stirring frequently, until the chocolate has melted and is smooth. Remove from the heat and leave for about 10 minutes or until the chocolate begins to thicken slightly.

Cut the fruit loaf into medium to thick slices, then spread with the melted chocolate. Leave until almost set, then cut each slice in half to form a triangle. Layer the chocolate-coated bread slices and the chopped apricots in the buttered ovenproof dish.

Stir the cream and the milk together, then stir in the caster sugar. Beat the eggs, then gradually beat in the cream and milk mixture. Beat thoroughly until well blended. Carefully pour over the bread slices and apricots and leave to stand for 30 minutes.

Sprinkle with the demerara sugar and place in a roasting tin half filled with boiling water. Cook in the preheated oven for 45 minutes, or until golden and the custard is lightly set. Serve immediately.

Rum Chocolate Squares

Makes 14–16

125 g/4 oz butter
100 g/3¹/₂ oz caster sugar
pinch salt
2 medium egg yolks
225 g/8 oz plain flour
50 g/2 oz cornflour
¹/₄ tsp baking powder
2 tbsp cocoa powder
1 tbsp rum

Preheat the oven to 190°C/350°F/Gas Mark 5, 10 minutes before baking. Lightly oil several baking sheets. Cream the butter, sugar and salt together in a large bowl until light and fluffy. Add the egg yolks and beat well until smooth.

Sift together 175 g/6 oz of the flour, the cornflour and the baking powder and add to the mixture and mix well with a wooden spoon until a smooth and soft dough is formed.

Halve the dough and knead the cocoa powder into one-half and the rum and the remaining plain flour into the other half. Place the two mixtures in two separate bowls, cover with clingfilm and chill in the refrigerator for 1 hour.

Roll out both pieces of dough separately on a well floured surface into two thin rectangles. Place one on top of the other, cut out squares approximately 5 cm/2 inch x 5 mm/¹/₄ inch and place on the prepared baking sheets.

Bake in the preheated oven, half with the chocolate uppermost and the other half, rum side up, for 10–12 minutes or until firm. Remove from the oven and leave to cool slightly. Using a spatula, transfer to a wire rack and leave to cool, then serve.

Coconut Macaroons

Makes 18

rice paper
2 medium egg whites
125 g/4 oz icing sugar
125 g/4 oz desiccated coconut
125 g/4 oz ground almonds
zest of ½ lemon or lime,
finely grated

Preheat the oven to 180°C/350°F/Gas Mark 4. Line two baking sheets with rice paper.

Whisk the egg whites in a clean, dry bowl until soft peaks form. Using a large metal spoon, fold in the icing sugar. Fold in the coconut, almonds and lemon or lime zest to make a sticky dough.

Heap dessertspoonfuls of the mixture onto the rice paper on the baking sheets. Bake for 10 minutes, then reduce the oven temperature to 150°C/300°F/Gas Mark 2.

Bake for a further 5–8 minutes until firm and golden, then remove to a wire rack to cool, breaking off any excess rice paper.

Chocolate Rum Truffles

Makes 44

For the chocolate truffles:

225 g/8 oz dark chocolate
25 g/1 oz butter, softened
2 medium egg yolks
2 tsp brandy or kirsch
2 tsp double cream
24 maraschino cherries, drained
2 tbsp cocoa powder, sifted

For the rum truffles:

125 g/4 oz dark chocolate
2 tbsp rum
125 ml/4 fl oz double cream
50 g/2 oz ground almonds
2 tbsp icing sugar, sifted

For the chocolate truffles, break the chocolate into pieces and place in a heatproof bowl set over a saucepan of gently simmering water. Leave for 20 minutes or until the chocolate has melted. Stir until the chocolate is smooth and remove from the heat. Leave to stand for about 6 minutes.

Beat the butter, the egg yolks, the brandy or kirsch and double cream together until smooth. Stir the melted chocolate into the butter and egg yolk mixture and stir until thick. Cover and leave to cool for about 30 minutes. Chill in the refrigerator for 1 1/2 hours or until firm.

Divide the truffle mixture into 24 and mould around the drained cherries. Roll in the cocoa powder until evenly coated. Place the truffles in petit four paper cases and chill in the refrigerator for 2 hours before serving.

To make the rum truffles, break the chocolate into small pieces and place in a heavy-based saucepan with the cream and rum. Heat gently until the chocolate has melted, then stir until smooth. Stir in the ground almonds and pour into a small bowl and chill in the refrigerator for at least 6 hours or until the mixture is thick.

Remove the mixture from the refrigerator and shape small spoonfuls into cherry-sized balls. Roll in the sifted icing sugar and place in petit four paper cases. Store the truffles in the refrigerator until ready to serve.

Orange Freeze

Serves 4

4 large oranges
1 small ripe mango, peeled, stoned
and chopped
about 300 ml/10 fl oz vanilla ice cream
225 g/8 oz raspberries
75 g/3 oz icing sugar, sifted,
plus extra for dusting
redcurrant sprigs, to decorate

Set the freezer to rapid-freeze. Using a sharp knife, carefully cut the lid off each orange. Scoop out the flesh from the orange, discarding any pips and thick pith. Place the shells and lids in the freezer, and chop any remaining orange flesh. Purée the mango flesh until smooth, then whisk together with the orange juice, orange flesh and vanilla ice cream until well blended. Pour into a shallow flat container.

Cover and freeze for about 2 hours, occasionally breaking up the ice crystals with a fork or a whisk. Stir the mixture from around the edge of the container into the centre, then level and return to the freezer. Do this two or three times, then leave until almost frozen solid.

Place a large scoop of the ice cream mixture into the frozen orange shells. Add another scoop on top, so that there is plenty outside of the orange shell, and return to the freezer for 1 hour. Arrange the lids on top and freeze for a further 2 hours, until the filled orange shell is completely frozen solid.

Meanwhile, using a nylon sieve, press the raspberries into a bowl using the back of a spoon and mix together with the icing sugar. Spoon the raspberry coulis onto 4 serving plates and place an orange at the centre of each one. Dust with extra icing sugar and serve decorated with the redcurrants. Remember to return the freezer to its normal setting.

Mango Sorbet

Serves 4

2 large ripe mangoes
2 or 3 limes (to give 3–4 tbsp juice)
50 g/2 oz granulated sugar
2 medium egg whites

Turn the freezer to rapid-freeze at least 1 hour before freezing. Peel the mango and cut in half on either side of the stone. Dice into small pieces. Blend in a food processor to form a smooth purée. Squeeze the limes and add to the processor, then blend for 1 minute. Scrape the purée into a bowl.

Put the sugar and 150 ml/5 fl oz water in a heavy-based saucepan and heat gently until the sugar has dissolved. Bring to the boil and boil steadily for 5 minutes, or until a light syrup is formed. Cool slightly, then stir into the mango purée.

Whisk the egg whites until soft peaks are formed, then stir into the mango mixture. Pour into a freezable container and freeze for 1 hour.

Stir the mango mixture to break up any ice crystals. Return to the freezer and freeze for a further 1 hour. Repeat the stirring and freezing once more, then leave in the freezer for 2 hours, or until frozen. Serve in scoops.

Tipsy Tropical Fruit

Serves 4

225 g/8 oz can pineapple chunks in
natural juice
2 guavas
1 papaya
2 passion fruit
25 g/1 oz unsalted butter
1 tbsp orange juice
50 g/2 oz creamed coconut,
chopped
50 g/2 oz soft light brown sugar
2 tbsp Malibu liqueur or white rum
fresh mint sprigs, to decorate
vanilla ice cream, to serve

Drain the pineapple chunks, reserving the juice. Pat the pineapple dry on absorbent kitchen paper. Peel the guavas and cut into wedges. Halve the papaya and scoop out the black seeds. Peel and cut into 2.5 cm/1 inch chunks. Halve the passion fruit and scoop out the pulp into a small bowl.

Heat the butter in a wok, add the pineapple and stir-fry over a high heat for 30 seconds. Reduce the heat and add the guava and papaya. Drizzle over the orange juice and cook for 2 minutes, stirring occasionally, taking care not to break up the fruit.

Using a slotted spoon, remove the fruit from the wok, leaving any juices behind, and transfer to a warmed serving dish. Add the creamed coconut to the wok with the sugar and reserved pineapple juice. Simmer for 2–3 minutes, stirring until the coconut has melted.

Add the Malibu or white rum to the wok and heat through, then pour over the fruit. Spoon the passion fruit pulp on top and serve hot with spoonfuls of ice cream, decorated with a sprig of mint.

Caramelised Oranges
in an Iced Bowl

Serves 4

For the ice bowl:

about 36 ice cubes
fresh flowers and fruits

8 medium-sized oranges
225 g/8 oz caster sugar
4 tbsp Grand Marnier,
Curaçao or Cointreau

Set the freezer to rapid-freeze. Place a few ice cubes in the base of a 1.7 litre/3 pint freezable glass bowl. Place a 900 ml/1¹/₂ pint glass bowl on top of the ice cubes. Arrange the flower heads and fruits in between the two bowls, wedging in position with the ice cubes. Weigh down the smaller bowl with some heavy weights, then carefully pour cold water between the two bowls making sure that the flowers and the fruit are covered. Freeze for at least 6 hours, or until the ice is frozen solid.

When ready, remove the weights and, using a hot damp cloth, rub the inside of the smaller bowl until it loosens sufficiently to remove. Place the larger bowl in a sink half-filled with very hot water. Leave for about 30 seconds, or until the ice loosens. Do not to leave in the water for too long or the ice will melt. Remove the bowl and leave in the refrigerator. Return the freezer to its normal setting.

Thinly pare the zest from 2 of the oranges, then cut into matchsticks. Using a sharp knife, cut away the zest and pith from all the oranges, catching the juices in a bowl. Slice the oranges, discarding pips, and re-form each into its original shape. Secure with cocktail sticks, then place in a bowl. Heat 300 ml/10 fl oz water with the orange zest and sugar in a pan. Stir until the sugar has dissolved. Bring to the boil. Boil for 15 minutes until a caramel colour. Remove the pan from the heat. Stir in the liqueur and pour over the oranges. Allow to cool. Chill for 3 hours, turning the oranges occasionally. Spoon into the ice bowl and serve.

Rice Pudding

Serves 4

60 g/2¹/₂ oz pudding rice
50 g/2 oz granulated sugar
410 g can coconut milk
300 ml/¹/₂ pint milk
pinch freshly grated nutmeg
1 tsp allspice
25 g/1 oz butter
jam, to decorate

Preheat the oven to 150°C/300°F/Gas Mark 2. Lightly oil a large ovenproof dish. Sprinkle the rice and the sugar into the dish and mix.

Bring the coconut milk and milk to the boil in a small pan, stirring occasionally. Stir the milks into the rice and mix well until the rice is coated thoroughly. Sprinkle over the nutmeg and allspice, cover with foil and bake in the preheated oven for 30 minutes.

Remove the pudding from the oven and stir well, breaking up any lumps. Cover with the same foil. Bake in the preheated oven for a further 30 minutes. Remove from the oven and stir well again. Dot the pudding with butter and bake for a further 45–60 minutes, until the rice is tender and the skin is browned.

Divide the pudding into four individual serving bowls. Top with a large spoonful of the jam and serve immediately.

Flan

Serves 4

125 g/4 oz caster sugar
150 ml/¹/₄ pint water
3 medium eggs
1 tsp vanilla extract
450 ml/³/₄ pint milk

Preheat the oven to 160°C/325°F/Gas Mark 3, 10 minutes before cooking. Place all but 1 tablespoon of the sugar in a heavy-based saucepan and add the water. Bring to the boil over a medium heat, stirring frequently in order to dissolve the sugar. When the sugar is completely dissolved, bring to the boil, then boil steadily until the syrup becomes golden.

Remove from the heat and quickly pour into four 150 ml/¹/₄ pint ramekins or ovenproof dishes. Working quickly, swirl the syrup around the dishes until they are lightly coated. It is advisable to use a thick cloth, as the dishes will be hot. Place in a roasting tin and reserve.

Beat the eggs together with the remaining sugar and the vanilla extract. Warm the milk slightly, then whisk or beat into the eggs. Carefully strain into the dishes in the roasting tin. Carefully pour in sufficient boiling water to go halfway up the sides of the dishes. Take care while placing in the oven and cook for 30–35 minutes until the custard has set and feels firm on the top. Remove and cool, then place in the refrigerator and leave to chill, preferably overnight.

When ready to serve, run a knife around the edge of each pudding and invert onto a serving dish.

Stir-fried Bananas Peaches with Rum Butterscotch Sauce

Serves 4

2 medium-firm bananas
1 tbsp caster sugar
2 tsp lime juice
4 firm, ripe peaches or nectarines
1 tbsp sunflower oil

For the rum butterscotch sauce:

50 g/2 oz unsalted butter
50 g/2 oz soft light brown sugar
125 g/4 oz demerara sugar
300 ml/¹/₂ pint double cream
2 tbsp dark rum

Peel the bananas and cut into 2.5 cm/1 inch diagonal slices. Place in a bowl and sprinkle with the caster sugar and lime juice and stir until lightly coated. Reserve.

Place the peaches or nectarines in a large bowl and pour over boiling water to cover. Leave for 30 seconds, then plunge them into cold water and peel off their skins. Cut each one into eight thick slices, discarding the stone.

Heat a wok, add the oil and swirl it round the wok to coat the sides. Add the fruit and cook for 3–4 minutes, shaking the wok and gently turning the fruit until lightly browned. Spoon the fruit into a warmed serving bowl and clean the wok with absorbent kitchen paper.

Add the butter and sugars to the wok and stir continuously over a very low heat until the sugar has dissolved. Remove from the heat and leave to cool for 2–3 minutes.

Stir the cream and rum into the sugar syrup and return to the heat. Bring to the boil and simmer for 2 minutes, stirring continuously until smooth. Leave for 2–3 minutes to cool slightly, then serve warm with the stir-fried peaches and bananas.

Drinks

The Caribbean is world-famous for its potent rum, which is often cheaper than water! Combined with a bounty of lush fresh tropical fruits ranging from the ugli fruit to the guava, there is no end of delicious drink combinations to be sampled. For a nonalcoholic pick-me-up why not try the thirst-quenching Revitalizing Creole Smoothie or the creamy Banana Ginger Cream? If you're celebrating or in need of a kick after a long day, shake up a Rum & Guava Fizz or a Cuba Libra.

Ugli Juice

Serves 1

1 ugli fruit
1 wedge ripe honeydew melon
few black seedless grapes
chilled sparkling water, to dilute
(optional)
extra grapes and mint sprig,
to decorate (optional)

Alternative:

Use either pink or red grapefruit
if ugli fruit is not available and, if
preferred, strain through a fine
sieve to give a smooth juice.

Peel the ugli fruit, discarding the peel and pith.

Cut the flesh into chunks. Remove any seeds from the melon
and discard the skin.

Cut into chunks and add to the ugli. Pass through a juicer or
blender until the juice is formed.

Pour into the glass and dilute with water, if using.

Decorate the glass with a mint sprig and a few grapes, if
using, by hanging little bunches over the rim of the glass.

Mango Orange Juice

Serves 1

2 large ripe mangos
2 large oranges
chilled sparkling water, to dilute
(optional)
ice cubes, to serve
thinly pared orange zest and mint
sprig, to decorate

Alternative:

Canned mangos can be used
if ripe ones are not available.
Drain before using. Ripe
papayas can also be used,
but discard the skin and
black seeds before juicing.

Peel the mangos and cut the flesh away from the large stone. Cut the flesh into chunks.

Using a vegetable peeler, carefully pare off two long thin strips of orange zest and reserve.

Peel the remaining zest and bitter white pith off both oranges and divide into segments.

Discard the pips and add to the mangos. Pass through a juicer or blender until the juice is formed.

Pour into the glass, dilute with water, if using, and add ice cubes.

Drape the orange zest down the sides of the glass, add the mint sprig and serve.

Tropical Fruit Juice

Serves 2

1 ripe mango
1 papaya
1 ripe passion fruit
$^1/_2$ medium, ripe pineapple
chilled mineral water, to
dilute (optional)
ice cubes, to serve
mint sprigs, to decorate

Alternative:

For a thicker, creamier juice,
add 1 large ripe peeled
banana before juicing.

Peel the mango and cut the flesh away from the stone.

Discard the peel and seeds from the papaya and cut into chunks.
Add to the mango.

Remove the plume and skin from the pineapple and cut lengthways
into four. Discard the hard central core and cut into chunks. Reserve
2–4 pieces and add the remainder to the mango and papaya.

Pass the fruits through a juicer or blender until the juice is formed.
Pour into glasses and dilute with water, if using.

Add ice cubes and decorate the glasses with the reserved
pineapple and mint sprigs. Serve.

Tropical Delight

Serves 2

1 large ripe mango
1 large ripe papaya
2 ripe bananas, peeled and cut
into chunks
juice of ¹/₂ lime
2–3 tsp clear honey
300 ml/¹/₂ pint coconut milk
ice cubes, to serve
lime slice, to decorate

Alternative:

Replace the coconut
milk with Greek yogurt and
sprinkle the top with a
little ground cinnamon.

Peel the mango and papaya and discard the stone and seeds.

Chop the fruits into large chunks and pour over the lime juice, then place all the ingredients to be blended in a smoothie machine or blender.

If using a smoothie machine, blend on mix for 15 seconds and then on smooth for 30 seconds. In a blender, blend for 1–2 minutes.

Place some ice cubes into a tall glass and add the prepared drink. Decorate and serve immediately.

Banana with Ginger Cream

Serves 2

2 large ripe bananas
2 large oranges
300 ml/¹/₂ pint coconut milk
6 ice cubes
2 tbsp whipped double cream,
to serve
1 tsp ginger (grated fresh root or
ground), to decorate
1 tsp crystallized ginger, chopped, to
decorate

Alternative:

Replace 1 of the bananas
with 175 g/6 oz peeled
and stoned lychees.

Peel the bananas and cut into chunks. Peel the oranges, discard the pith and divide into segments.

Place all the ingredients to be blended, including the ice, in a smoothie machine or blender.

If using a smoothie machine, blend on mix for 15 seconds and then on smooth for 30 seconds. In a blender, blend for 1–2 minutes.

Mix the cream and ginger together and stir half into the drink. Pour into glasses, top with the remaining cream and the crystallized ginger and serve.

Revitalizing Creole Smoothie

Serves 2

50 ml/2 fl oz lime juice
300 ml/^{1}/$_2$ pint orange juice
175 g/6 oz carrots,
peeled and chopped
75 g/3 oz okra,
trimmed and chopped
225 g/8 oz tomatoes, chopped
4 spring onions,
trimmed and chopped
1 tbsp rolled oats
4 ice cubes
basil leaves, trimmed spring onions,
and tomatoes, to decorate
2 cleaned and trimmed celery
stalks with leaves still attached,
for stirring (optional)

Alternative:

Add 1 deseeded and chopped chilli
before blending or use a few dashes
Tabasco sauce to spice it up and
kick-start your day.

Place all the ingredients to be blended in a smoothie machine or blender.

If using a smoothie machine, blend on mix for 15 seconds and then on smooth for 45 seconds. In a blender, blend for 1–2 minutes until smooth.

Pour into glasses, decorate with the basil leaves, trimmed spring onions and tomatoes and serve immediately with the trimmed celery stalks for stirring, if using.

Virgin Raspberry Daiquiri

Serves 1

1 tsp caster sugar
3 measures raspberry syrup or
fresh fruit purée
2 measures pineapple juice
$^1/_2$ measure lemon juice
4 ice cubes, crushed
lemonade, to top up
fresh raspberries threaded onto a
cocktail stick and mint sprig,
to decorate

Alternative:

Replace the raspberry syrup
with cranberry juice and
the pineapple juice
with mango juice.

Place the caster sugar into a saucer and place some water in another saucer.

Dip the rim of a chilled glass into the water and then into the sugar. Turn the rim until well coated in the sugar, then chill until required.

Pour the raspberry syrup or fresh fruit purée into a cocktail shaker or jug and add the pineapple and lemon juice. Shake or stir until well blended.

Place the crushed ice into the sugared glass and pour over the blended drink. Top up with lemonade, decorate and serve.

Frozen Daiquiri

Serves 1

For sugar syrup:

225 g/8 oz white granulated sugar
150 ml/¹/₄ pint water

For the drink:

4 ice cubes, crushed
freshly squeezed juice from
2 ripe limes
1 tsp sugar syrup (see above)
2 measures white rum
lime wedge, to decorate

Alternative:

Try a Melon Daiquiri by
adding 2 measures Midori
(Melon Liqueur) and only
use 1 measure of freshly
squeezed lime juice.

To make sugar syrup, place the sugar and water in a heavy-based saucepan and place over a gentle heat. Heat gently, stirring occasionally, until the sugar has completely dissolved. Bring to the boil and boil steadily (to a temperature of 105˚C/221˚F) until a light syrup is formed. Remove from the heat. Leave to cool, then pour into a screw-top sterilized bottle. When cold, screw down the lid. Use as required. It is better used fresh, as after a while it could begin to crystallize.

To make the daiquiri, place the crushed ice into a cocktail shaker and pour in the lime juice, 1 teaspoon sugar syrup and white rum.

Shake for 1 minute, or until the shaker feels very cold.

Strain into the chilled glass. Serve decorated with the lime wedge.

Rum Planter Cocktail

Serves 1

4 ice cubes, crushed
1 measure dark rum
1 tsp freshly squeezed
orange juice
1 tsp freshly squeezed
lemon juice
2 dashes Angostura bitters
1 tsp caster sugar
tropical fruits, to decorate, such as
pineapple, cherry and lime

Alternative:

Vary the fruits used to decorate.
For a special occasion, make a
stunning decorate by threading small
pieces of mango, kiwi, pineapple and
papaya onto a short kebab stick
and balance across the glass.

Place the crushed ice into a cocktail shaker and add
the rum with the orange and lemon juices, together
with the Angostura bitters and sugar.

Shake for 1 minute, or until a frost is formed on the
outside of the shaker.

Pour into a tumbler and decorate with small pieces of
pineapple, cherry and lime.

Bacardi Classic

Serves 1

1¹/₂–2 measures Bacardi rum
1 measure lemon juice
1 tsp grenadine
1 tsp, or to taste, sugar syrup
(*see* page 218)
2 ice cubes, crushed
1 maraschino cherry
lime wedge

Alternative:

Use the 2 measures
Bacardi rum if a stronger
drink is preferred, and replace
the lemon juice with lime juice.

Place all the ingredients into a cocktail shaker and shake for 30 seconds.

Pour into a cocktail glass and serve decorated with the cherry and lime wedge.

Brandy Classic

Serves 1

1 measure brandy
1 measure blue Curaçao
1 tbsp freshly squeezed lemon juice
1 tbsp syrup from a jar of
maraschino cherries
3 ice cubes, crushed
lemon zest spiral, to decorate

Alternative:

Try replacing the brandy
with either gin or vodka
or even white rum.

Place the ingredients into a cocktail shaker and shake for 30 seconds.

Pour into a cocktail glass and serve decorated with the lemon zest spiral.

Scorpio

Serves 1

5 ice cubes, crushed
1 measure brandy
$^1/_2$ measure white rum
$^1/_2$ measure dark rum
2 measures freshly squeezed
orange juice
$^1/_2$ measure Amaretto Disaronno
2–3 dashes Angostura bitters

Alternative:

Use all dark or white rum,
if preferred.

Place half the crushed ice into a cocktail shaker and add the brandy, white and dark rum, orange juice, Amaretto Disaronno and Angostura bitters.

Shake for 1 minute, or until a frost is formed on the outside of the shaker.

Strain into a glass, add the remaining crushed ice and serve with a stirrer.

Mojito

Serves 1

4 ice cubes, crushed
2–3 mint sprigs
2 measures white rum
3 tbsp freshly squeezed lime juice
2 tsp, or to taste, demerara sugar
soda water
fresh mint sprig, to decorate

Alternative:

Try using other flavoured
rums, such as dark rum, or
even fruit-flavoured rums,
such as mango-flavoured.

Place half the crushed ice into a glass and add the mint
sprigs. Carefully crush the mint on the ice.

Pour the rum, lime juice, sugar and remaining ice into
a cocktail shaker and shake until a frost forms on the
outside of the shaker.

Pour into the glass, top up with soda water, decorate with
a fresh mint sprig and serve with a stirrer.

White Witch

Serves 1

4 ice cubes
1–2 measures white rum
$^1/_2$ measure white crème de cacao
$^1/_2$ measure Cointreau
1 tbsp lime juice
soda water, to top up
lime slice, to decorate

Alternative:

Make a Red Witch cocktail.
Simply place crushed ice into
a tall glass, add 1 measure
Pernod and 2 measures
blackcurrant cordial. Top
up with cider and serve.

Place half the ice cubes into a cocktail shaker with the white rum, crème de cacao and Cointreau.

Add the lime juice, then shake for 30 seconds.

Place the remaining ice cubes in an 'old-fashioned glass' (this is a stubby glass with a thick base, which holds about 230 ml/8 fl oz, and was the original glass for cocktails to be served in), then strain the cocktail into the glass.

Top up with soda water and serve decorated with a lime slice.

Rum Guava Fizz

Serves 2–3

3 ripe guavas
6 measures rum, preferably
white rum
2 measures pineapple juice
crushed ice
$^1/_2$ bottle sparkling white wine

Alternative:

Replace the sparkling wine
with sparkling apple juice,
lemonade or mineral water
and use a few dashes
Angostura bitters in
place of the rum.

Peel the guavas and discard the seeds.

Pass through a juicer into a jug, then stir in the rum and pineapple juice.

Place some crushed ice into tall glasses, pour over the guava mixture, top up with the sparkling wine and serve.

Cuba Libre

Serves 1

1 tbsp freshly squeezed,
strained lime juice
3 ice cubes, crushed
2 measures Bacardi rum
5 measures cola
orange spiral, to decorate

Alternative:

Replace the Bacardi rum
with dark rum and use orange
juice in place of the lime juice.

Cut the squeezed lime shell in half and place in a chilled highball glass (this glass is a tall tumbler and holds 280 ml/10 fl oz).

Pour the lime juice into the glass.

Spoon in the ice, then pour over the rum and top up with the cola.

Add a straw and a swizzle stick and decorate with an orange spiral.

Caribbean Sunset

Serves 1

3 ice cubes
1 measure crème de banane
$^1/_2$ measure blue Curaçao
$^1/_2$ measure freshly squeezed
lemon juice
$^1/_2$ measure mango juice
2 tbsp whipped cream
1 tsp grenadine
star fruit slice, small mango or
strawberry wedge, to decorate

Alternative:

Try adding $^1/_2$ measure
gin for more bite.

Place a couple of the ice cubes into a cocktail shaker and the remaining ice into a short glass.

Pour the crème de banane into the cocktail shaker together with the blue Curaçao, the lemon and mango juices and half the whipped cream.

Shake for 30 seconds, or until blended. Pour over the ice cubes and add the grenadine, allowing it to sink slowly.

Top with the remaining cream, decorate and serve.

Tropical Bubbles

Serves 2

1 large ripe mango
1 large ripe papaya
2 ripe guavas
6 measures pineapple juice
$1/2$ bottle chilled champagne or sparkling wine
mint sprigs, to decorate (optional)
2 pineapple wedges, to decorate (optional)

Alternative:

For a nonalcoholic version, omit the champagne and use sparkling spring water or lemonade.

Peel the mango, papaya and guavas and discard the stone and seeds. Cut into chunks.

Place in a blender and add the pineapple juice. Whizz for 1–2 minutes until smooth, then pour into chilled tall glasses and top up with champagne.

Serve with a stirrer, if liked, and decorate with mint sprigs and pineapple wedges.

Piña Colada

Serves 1

4 ice cubes, crushed
1 measure white rum
2 measures coconut cream
2 measures pineapple juice
pineapple wedge, pineapple leaves
and maraschino cherry, to decorate

Alternative:

Make a 'Chi Chi', the Hawaiian
version of the Piña Colada, by
substituting vodka for the rum.

Place the crushed ice into a cocktail shaker and pour in the white rum, coconut cream and pineapple juice.

Shake for 20 seconds, or until well blended.

Strain into a tall glass and decorate with the pineapple wedge and cherry and serve with a straw.

Tobago Fizz

Serves 1

4 ice cubes
1 tbsp freshly squeezed lime juice
2 tbsp freshly squeezed orange juice
3 measures golden or white rum
1 measure single cream
$^1/_2$ tsp clear honey
soda water, to top up
strawberry, to decorate

Alternative:

For an extra kick, replace the
soda water with sparkling wine.

Place the ice cubes into a cocktail shaker and pour in the lime and orange juices.

Add the rum with the single cream and honey.

Shake for 45 seconds, or until a frost forms on the outside of the cocktail shaker.

Strain into a tall stemmed glass, top up with soda water and serve decorated with a strawberry.

Island Affair

Serves 1

3 ice cubes, crushed
1 measure Midori
(melon liqueur)
1–1¹/2 measures Cointreau
¹/2 measure blue Curaçao
1¹/2 measures freshly squeezed
orange juice
2 measures mango juice
1 tbsp lightly whipped cream
mango slice, pineapple
slice or melon wedge,
to decorate

Place the crushed ice into a tall glass. Pour the Midori into a cocktail shaker, together with the Cointreau, blue Curaçao and the fruit juices.

Shake for 30 seconds, or until blended, then strain over the crushed ice.

Float the whipped cream on top and serve decorated with your choice of fruits and a stirrer.

Creole Punch

Serves 10–12

12 ice cubes, crushed
1 bottle port
6 measures, or to taste, brandy
3 measures freshly squeezed
lemon juice
lemonade, to top up
orange and lemon half-moon and
kiwi slices, to decorate

Alternative:

Make a single glass in the
same method and using the
following amounts: 4 ice cubes,
crushed; 2 measures port;
½ measure brandy and
2 teaspoons freshly
squeezed lemon juice.
Decorate as above.

Place the crushed ice into punchbowl and pour over the port and brandy.

Add the lemon juice, then stir well.

Pour into glasses and top up with the lemonade.

Spear the orange, lemon and kiwi slices onto a cocktail stick and serve with a stirrer and straw.

Caribbean Toddy

Serves 2

5 measures white rum
1 tsp demerara sugar
150 ml/¼ pint boiling water
6 drops Angostura bitters
½ tsp finely grated lime zest
2 lime twists, to decorate
freshly grated nutmeg, to decorate

Alternative:

For a nonalcoholic version,
replace the white rum with
freshly brewed, hot black tea.

Pour the white rum into a blender or cocktail shaker and add the sugar.

Pour over the boiling water and blend or shake until the sugar has dissolved.

Add the Angostura bitters and lime zest and shake again until mixed.

Pour into heatproof glasses, add a lime twist to each, sprinkle with a little grated nutmeg and serve.

Bahamas Punch

Serves 12

125 g/4 oz, or to taste, light
muscovado sugar
300 ml/¹/₂ pint water
1 lemon, preferably organic
3 small oranges, preferably organic
300 ml/¹/₂ pint cold strong
black tea
1 bottle (70 cl) dark rum
fresh pineapple wedges and orange
spirals, to decorate

Alternative:

Use white rum in place
of the dark rum and add a
little fresh pineapple to
the bowl before heating.

Place the sugar into a heavy-based saucepan and pour in the water.

Thinly pare the zest from the lemon and 1 of the oranges and add to the saucepan.

Heat gently, stirring frequently, for 12–15 minutes until the sugar has dissolved.

Bring to the boil and boil for 5 minutes, then remove from the heat.

Squeeze out the juice from all the fruits and add to the saucepan together with the tea and rum.

Stir, then strain into heatproof glasses, decorate and serve.

Tropical Cup

Serves 16

300 ml/^{1}/$_2$ pint dark rum
250 ml/8^1/$_2$ fl oz apricot brandy
300 ml/^{1}/$_2$ pint pineapple juice
300 ml/^{1}/$_2$ pint freshly squeezed
pink grapefruit juice
6 measures freshly squeezed
orange juice
8 measures mango juice
3 ripe passion fruits
10 ice cubes, crushed
1 small ripe mango and
12–16 maraschino cherries,
to decorate

Alternative:

Add more tropical fruits to the
cup. Try chopped papaya,
pineapple and mango. Do not
throw the fruit away; serve with
ice cream as a luscious dessert.

Pour the rum and brandy into a punchbowl and stir in all
the fruit juices.

Scoop out the flesh, seeds and juice from the passion
fruits and stir into the bowl together with the crushed ice.

Peel and stone the mango, then cut into small dice and stir
into the punch together with the maraschino cherries.
Serve in heatproof glasses decorated with cherries.

Index